Managing Change

Managing Change

The Strategies of Making Change Work for You

JOHN S. MORGAN

Consultant-Labor Resources
General Electric Company

McGRAW-HILL BOOK COMPANY

New York   St. Louis   San Francisco   Düsseldorf   Johannesburg
Kuala Lumpur   London   Mexico   Montreal   New Delhi
Panama   Rio de Janeiro   Singapore   Sydney   Toronto

Library of Congress Cataloging in Publication Data

Morgan, John Smith, 1921–
  Managing change: the strategies of making change
work for you.

  1. Management.   2. Technological innovations.
3. Organizational change.   I. Title.
HD45.M67   658.4'06   74-39049
ISBN 0-07-043114-0

MANAGING CHANGE

123456789 BPBP 765432

The editors for this book were W. Hodson Mogan,
Don A. Douglas, and Karen Kesti, the designer
was Naomi Auerbach, and its production was
supervised by Teresa F. Leaden. It was set in
Linofilm Baskerville by Vail-Ballou Press, Inc.

It was printed and bound by The Book Press.

To my father-in-law, Stanley L. Willis

Contents

Preface

More change has occurred in our way of life since 1900 than in the previous 1900 years. Managers and professionals in business, industry, or government—from supervisor of a small component within the organization to chief executive officer—must learn to take change into account as a continuing factor in their working existence.

In the future, even more dramatic change appears likely. Therefore, the manager or professional who deals with change most effectively will fare the best in his career. The purpose of this book is to outline techniques and strategies that can help to meet this challenge, particularly in the areas of technology, methods, organization, and people.

Changes interact. A change that is primarily technological may force profound, but largely unforeseen, organizational shifts.

Or a relatively minor change in the method of doing things—in the approach to selling, for example—may result in disturbing changes for people. A goal of *Managing Change* is to alert readers to the phenomenon of interaction.

It has become a truism that many established companies have missed the boat with new technologies. For example, at least two major firms knew about, but failed to pursue, xerography. This book outlines strategies that a manager can pursue to monitor his field for coming technological change and to follow those developments most promising for his operation.

Presented in *Managing Change* are ways to use methods change so that a person may help his company, his career, or that of those who work for or with him. Example: Instituting changes in job design that make employees' work more challenging.

In managing change in the organization, the strategy is to know how to spot the need for it, how to judge when it isn't necessary, and how to know what result you want the change to accomplish.

Man generates changes in technology, methods, and organization, but probably the most complex change the reader will ever deal with is transformation in people themselves. "People change" occurs on at least two levels—in mores and in psychological mutations in individuals, due to age, changes in their environment, and other factors. This book suggests ways of minimizing the problems that arise when such shifts occur.

Managing change effectively also requires more than technique and strategy. It calls for a new kind of thinking about change—as an element in planning, as a factor in all decision making, and as a pervading force in practically all other aspects of management. This book attempts to help readers consider change in the sense of an opportunity for self-motivation and progress, not in the context of displacement and disorder.

JOHN S. MORGAN

Managing Change

part one

Introduction

chapter one

Charting for Change

An artist won first prize for his drawing. In accepting the award, he remarked to the judge, "You know, this isn't my best work."

"Why didn't you submit your best, then?" asked the judge.

"Because I haven't done it yet," replied the artist.

None of us has done his best work—yet. But hopefully in the future we will do things better as we grow and improve and change. Change may connote—although it doesn't necessarily guarantee—improvement.

Nothing is ever completed. In managing change, managers particularly must never lose their tolerance for ambiguity—their recognition that all things change. To better the odds that change will indeed mean improvement, managers must try to direct the forces of change that come within their purview.

The object of this book is to help you manage change so that improvement will occur—in the technology of your operation, in the methods you use to get things done, in the organization you adopt to maximize your effectiveness, and in people who work for and with you.

We have experienced more technological change in the past twenty years than we did in the previous two hundred. We see dimly before us the prospects of change that may be more profound than anything faced by man since he left his cave. Two aspects about present change particularly disturb most of us—its speed and its profundity. Of course, change is and always has been part of the job of living and surviving. What we are experiencing is the speed-up of an already electrifying rate of change— accelerating acceleration. To show you how fast the rate of change has been accelerating, suppose you could compress the last fifty thousand years into fifty years. This is how those fifty years in the history of human civilization would look:

- Fifty years ago Neanderthal man was in his prime.
- Ten years ago he stopped living in caves.
- Five years ago he began to communicate with other people by means of picture writing.
- Six months ago the printing press was invented.
- One month ago the electric lamp was invented.
- Three weeks ago the Wright brothers flew the first airplane.
- A week and a half ago the first jet plane was flown.
- One week ago television sets were sold to the public for the first time.
- Yesterday the first American astronaut took a ride in space.
- A few seconds ago man landed on the moon.

With the pace of change being speeded at this rate, we can look forward—with excitement or trepidation—to even more fantastic developments in the remaining years of the twentieth century than we have seen in our lifetime to date.

The profundity of the changes now occurring is the second factor in the equation. Kenneth Boulding, an economist and social thinker, points out that a man born in 1900 now sees a kind of life as different from his youth as his youth was different from Julius Caesar's. Here are a few statistical measures of the profundity of change:

■ In 1850, four cities in the world had a population of 1 million or more. In 1900, there were nineteen; in 1960, 141. The world urban population is increasing at 6.5 per cent yearly, which will double the world cities' census in eleven years.

■ Half of the energy consumed by man in the past 2,000 years has been used in the last hundred.

■ Advanced nations are doubling their gross national products about every fifteen years. Within a seventy-year lifetime, five such doublings will take place. With compounding, a person in old age will have thirty-two times as much goods and services around him as when he was born.

Since 1946, statistics concerning the American economy show the dimensions of change:

■ Gross national product has grown two and a half times in real terms.

■ In the quarter century, United States manufacturers added as much to output as the total in all prior years since the industrial revolution began.

■ Americans in the twenty-five-year span had 50 per cent more money to spend (in real terms) although the population rose by just one-third.

If you extrapolate ahead for about another quarter century, the United States gross national product in constant dollars may reach $3 trillion by the year 2000, severely taxing our managerial and many other resources. By 2000, our annual increment in added GNP (in then-constant dollars) will near $300 billion—larger than our entire GNP in 1950.

What will economic change of this order mean to our way of life? We may get some kind of clue by looking at what has already changed recently. For example, more than half of the products now on our supermarket shelves weren't there a decade ago. Will there be a complete changeover—or more than one—in the next quarter century? Will the present supermarket as we know it even exist? Perhaps we will view the products in the comfort of our living room on the television screen, order the goods by punching buttons in our chair-side computer, pick up our packaged selections an hour later from a nearby distribution center easily reached in the electric auto we use in urban areas. Our selections may include a washing product as different from detergents as detergents are from the near-extinct soap flakes now. Milk will come in a plastic container because the paper carton will be as rare as the glass milk bottle is now. The ham is packaged in a substance which serves as the basting when we cook it in our electronic oven, as common in 2000 as the electric or gas cooking ovens of the 1970s. We don't buy edible products for more than one week ahead in 2000 because they are all packaged in materials which "self-destruct" after ten days. At the check-out station, we confirm the charges with the electronic indicator that gives our billing number. We need sign nothing, and the ball-point pen has become as unusual as a fountain pen is in the 1970s.

Included in our purchases are a paper dress to be worn at a forthcoming party and then discarded, new plastic bedroom curtains to replace the somewhat soiled set in use for the past quarter, and a booklet of architectural plans to provide ideas on how to rearrange the movable walls in the interior of our apartment.

Fanciful? Science fiction? Hardly. All the foregoing products, systems, and ideas are at least theoretically possible now. For a generation that has seen the silk stocking virtually disappear, the propeller-driven aircraft become almost as rare as the steam locomotive, and a typewriter nearly as ubiquitous as a pen, changes of this order should come as no surprise—and hardly any shock.

The shock—or "future shock" in the words of Alvin Toffler's

book of that title—comes in the scarcely noticed results of that change. One result is a new transience in our society. Examples:

■ Some 7,000 new product-brands found their way onto supermarket shelves in 1966, but most of them don't exist today.

■ Passenger miles traveled within the United States have been increasing at a rate six times faster than population for at least twenty-five years. Paved streets and roads have been built in the United States at a rate of 200 miles a day every day for the last twenty years.

■ Some 36.6 million Americans move their homes each year—as though the combined population of Turkey and Lebanon had all moved within a year.

■ In seventy major cities of the United States, including New York, the average residence in one place is just four years.

This transience finds expression in rapidly changing clothing styles, even for men. The phenomenon of fads—hula hoops, super balls, etc.—is symbolic of transience. At least one firm, Wham-O Manufacturing Company, actually specializes in fads. Temporary buildings, the trend toward renting cars and many other things, temporary help agencies—all these indicate transience and change. A recent survey of 1,000 business executives revealed that one-third of them occupied jobs that hadn't existed before. A survey of the Labor Department showed that 71 million people in the United States labor force held jobs for 4.2 years on the average, vs. 4.6 years on the average only three years earlier.

In the early 1960s, another Labor Department survey showed a man in his early twenties could expect to change jobs six or seven times during his lifetime. Instead of thinking of a career, younger people are beginning to think of serial careers.

The job turnover rate today is the highest among engineers and scientists because this is where the greatest changes are taking place. The "half-life" of a top engineer may be about ten years—that is, about half of what he learned in school will be obsolete within a decade.

And government is changing. The forty-year period from 1913 to 1953 saw no cabinet-level changes in federal government. The Department of Health, Education and Welfare was formed in 1953, Housing and Urban Development in 1965, and Transportation in 1967. The British prime ministership has changed hands 13 per cent faster since 1922 than between 1721 and 1922.

Celebrities seem to pass through more quickly, also—Twiggy, the Beatles, John Glenn, Jackie Kennedy. Books are coming out more frequently but with shorter tenures on best-seller lists. Evidence is persuasive that even today's symphony orchestras play the music of Mozart and other classic composers at a faster tempo than when it was written. Of the 450,000 "usable" words in English today, Shakespeare would be able to understand only about 250,000, estimates Stuart Berg Flexner, senior editor of the *Random House Dictionary of the English Language.*[1] He believes most of the language turnover has occurred in the last half century.

Observers generally agree that the engine of much of this change is technology. And the driver of that engine is largely business—in the United States, the American corporation. American business is changing prodigiously. Some indications include these:

■ In 1948, capital stocks (structures and equipment) per worker in manufacturing were $6,600; $9,500 by 1966; and $15,000 in 1970. By 1975, the capital stocks per employee will be $17,000.

■ By 1975, the typical firm will have to add 35 per cent to sales capacity just to stay even.

■ At the end of World War II not more than 20 per cent of American companies attempted systematic technological forecasts beyond a three-year horizon. Now 90 per cent do. About 600

[1] Copyright 1966 by Random House, Inc., New York.

large and medium-sized American firms have established a special technological forecasting function on their central management staff, spending $100 million a year to look ten, twenty, and even thirty years ahead.

■ In the last 15 years, while GNP doubled, research and development soared 400 per cent in the United States.

■ Before World War II, American research and development never exceeded 0.5 per cent of GNP. In 1948 it was still under 1 per cent. It exceeded 1 per cent in 1952. It was over 3 per cent of GNP in 1969.

■ Between 1957 and 1967, when American industry doubled its research and development performance, basic research increased 125 per cent.

■ In every year since 1964, industrial-conducted and -financed research and development spending has increased more than United States government spending, doubling to $8 billion in 1968, the highest in the world.

■ The value of general-purpose computer installations has climbed in the United States from $4 billion in 1962, to $8 billion in 1965, to $14 billion in 1968, to an estimated $30 billion in 1972.

■ American companies have broadened their geographical horizons, too. Since 1955, American companies' direct business investment abroad has grown from $19 billion to more than $65 billion. At recent rates, it's increasing by an average of $10 million a day.

Changes on such a scale have both impressed and alarmed many world leaders in government, education, and business.

President Nixon has said, "The first responsibility of leadership is to gain mastery over events."

The late Charles de Gaulle has stated, "It so happens that the world is undergoing a transformation to which no change that has yet occurred can be compared either in scope or in rapidity."

The late Dr. Robert Oppenheimer, when he was director of Princeton's Institute for Advanced Study, expressed the break with former eras this way: "This world of ours is a new world, in which the unity of knowledge, the nature of human communities, the order of society, the order of ideas, the very notions of society and culture have changed, and will not return to what they have been in the past. What is new is not new because it has never been there before, but because it has changed in quality. One thing that is new is the prevalence of newness, the changing scale and scope of change itself, so that the world alters as we walk in it, so that the years of man's life measure not some small growth or rearrangement or moderation of what he learned in childhood, but a great upheaval."

Alvin Toffler [2] says, "We are increasing the rate at which we must form and forget our images of reality. . . . Change is the process by which the future invades our lives."

Dr. Robert Hilliard, the top educational-broadcasting specialist for the Federal Communications Commission, makes this point: "At the rate at which knowledge is growing, by the time the child born today graduates from college, the amount of knowledge in the world will be four times as great. By the time that same child is fifty years old, it will be 32 times as great, and 97 per cent of everything known in the world will have been learned since the time he was born."

Sir Geoffrey Vickers, British social scientist, believes, "The rate of change increases at an accelerating speed, without a corresponding acceleration in the rates at which further responses can be made; and this brings us nearer the threshold beyond which control is lost."

General Lauris Norstad, chairman of Owens-Corning Fiberglas Corporation, has said, "The preservation of what we have known as the free-enterprise system will, in the longer term, depend on willingness and ability to adapt to change. . . . We must expect the 1970's to include a turning point of fundamental significance

[2] In *Future Shock,* copyright 1970 by Alvin Toffler, published by Random House, Inc., New York.

in contemporary history. Within this decade we should identify one of these critical periods when ideas germinate and decisions direct events, when man does not merely accept, he designs his destiny. Surely the challenge of these times is enormous, far greater, far more serious, far more complex than the challenge of any time in the past. But our ability to deal with the challenge has also grown tremendously. If there is one constant, it must in some way involve the nature of man, his capacity for constructive thought and effort—his conscience. And here, I am certain, is the real basis for confidence."

So, the dangers clearly are present, but so are the opportunities. How do ordinary people like you and me handle change? Most of us don't do anything about it. We sleep through it. The sleepers "manage" change by trying to ignore it, by refusing to acknowledge it, or by actually not realizing the scope and speed of it. The most common sleeper protests that things really aren't changing as much as they seem. "There's always been and always will be a generation gap," they often say. Of course there has. But the nature of today's generation gap is something unique because today's youth feel in their bones, as today's older people do not, the nature of the change now occurring.

A second common reaction to the change is, "It's inevitable." The inevitablists tend to the laissez-faire school. Nothing can be done. It's God's will. The inevitablists have something in common with the little old lady who refused to fly in a Boeing 747. "If God wanted me to fly in *that*," she said, "He wouldn't have provided the 707." The inevitablists tend to look on attempts to control change as unwarranted incursions into personal freedom.

A third common approach is hand wringing. Isn't all this change awful? What's the world coming to? The hand wringers tend to favor devices that attempt to stop or slow the clock. Many want tighter government controls. Many express alarm at automation. Some environmentalists have been persuaded that government control is the only answer to the negative results of technology. The answer is not less technology, but more, to counteract some of the bad effects. Furthermore, technology probably can't be stopped for long. If it is, dire consequences usually result.

A celebrated case involves the long-departed U.S. Electric Lighting Company. In the late 1870s and early 1880s, it was one of the leaders in its field. Having decided that it had all the change it could absorb comfortably, the company in 1881 pensioned off its leading inventor, Hiram Maxim, on condition that he pursue his activities outside the United States. Maxim went to England, where he developed many notable inventions, including the Maxim machine gun, famed in World War I. In the meantime, U.S. Electric lost $1.5 million between 1882 and 1889, when a competitor finally bought what was left of the company.

The fourth approach, and the one espoused here, is to try to control change within the limits of your purview or jurisdiction. The let's-do-it types accept change as inevitable, just as the inevitablists do, but they differ in that they believe something can be done to control some of this increasingly important aspect of twentieth-century life.

The let's-do-it people favor a pragmatic approach to change. First, they say, let's try to predict what is most likely to occur in a given area in the future. Let's appraise what effect or effects it will have on our operation. Let's decide what result is most desirable. Finally, let's try to devise ways and means of maximizing the chances that the most desired alternative will indeed come about.

chapter two

Preparing for Change — I

Consider the stirrup and the transistor. The comparison between the ancient and modern invention can give us new insights into change.

The stirrup is a simple loop, usually of metal, suspended by an adjustable strap from the side of a saddle, enabling the rider to mount and ride an animal, usually a horse, more easily.

Stirrups are mentioned in early Chinese literature, and examples that are probably earlier than the seventh century A.D. have been found in Japan. Yet the ingenious Greeks and Romans evidently knew nothing of them because there's no indication that they used them. The earliest sign of European use is not until the seventh century. In Europe, however, the stirrup took another several hundred years before it came into common use.

Over that lengthy period, the stirrup revolutionized warfare.

Without stirrups, a man could not handle heavy weapons while on a horse, so the basic soldier remained on foot until the stirrup gave him the support to manipulate his spear, sword, and shield while on horseback. The Arabs developed the stirrup to its extremes, and it's no accident that the military success of the mounted Moslem troops coincided with the development of larger stirrups.

In self-defense, Europeans adopted the large stirrup—and acquired some of the larger Arabian horses. Further breeding developed an animal of the size and strength for heavy farm work, leading to a revolution in farming methods. Especially in Europe, the horse began to replace the slow-moving ox as the beast of burden and ploughing. Because the horse could cultivate larger areas than the ox, farming grew more productive.

This evolution led gradually to a change in living habits. The larger farms permitted people to live farther apart, spreading the population and starting to break up the ancient feudal clusters of living.

Yet all this took centuries to evolve. Contrast that evolution with the quarter-century history of the transistor. The device amplifies electrical signals by the action of electronic charge carriers within a semiconducting crystalline solid. Because transistors can be made small, long-lived and efficient, they find extensive use in electronic systems for such purposes as communication, automatic control, and high-speed computation.

The point-contact type of transistor was invented by John Bardeen and Walter Brattain in the course of a research program at Bell Telephone Laboratories in New Jersey, initiated after radar experience in World War II showed a need for better understanding of semiconductor devices. In the first five years after its announcement in 1948, the transistor found uses for many communications functions in radio and television receivers, sound and high-frequency amplifers, electronic computers, control systems, etc. Comparable in flexibility with the thermionic electron tube, its range of application supplements that of tubes by making feasible operation of electronic equipment in smaller sizes, consuming less power and with improved reliability, especially under conditions of high vibration or shock.

The transistor has brought the small, inexpensive radio to the African native, the Bedouin shepherd, and the Indian farmer. Such peoples, often illiterate or with scant access to written material, are listening for the first time to a world beyond their narrow circle. The results are still unfolding, but one is a spur to nationalism in the underdeveloped portion of the world as leaders use the radio to kindle national and ethnic pride.

For example, the transistor radio has made it possible for Radio Cairo to become the biggest broadcaster in the world, larger than China and Russia when you subtract the jamming. It broadcasts in twenty-seven dialects—from Oran to Istanbul to Yemen and even down to Madagascar—twenty-four hours a day. Cairo beams its voice at every village, water hole, oasis, and camel train. All the Arab world has its ears pressed to the transistor radio.

In a far more complex application, the computer, the transistor has helped to broaden greatly the use of that device. And the computer has had such far-reaching impact on today's world that we need not belabor it here, except to emphasize that today's world wouldn't be what it is without the transistorized computer.

THE CHANGING NATURE OF CHANGE

The stirrup helped lift man's body a few feet off the ground. The transistor helped lift man's mind. The stirrup and its ramifications took centuries to evolve. The transistor has probably generated as much or more change as the stirrup, but in only a quarter century. The stirrup is simple. By comparison, the transistor is complex. The mechanics of the stirrup have remained unchanged for centuries, although the need for it declines steadily as the machine—perhaps transistorized—supplants the horse. The transistor, even now, is being supplanted by related but more sophisticated semiconducting devices because the need for more and better of these electronic aids proliferates.

Among the many facets of change, five stand out in the stirrup-transistor comparison:

1. Both the stirrup and the transistor generated spin-off results, distinct in nature from the invention of the device itself.

2. Many of the spin-offs are nontechnological, even though the engines of those changes were basically technical.

3. The spin-offs come with accelerating acceleration as the years pass.

4. Many of the spin-off changes resulting from both the invention of the stirrup and the transistor were unforeseen at the time the devices were introduced.

5. As time passes, the spin-off changes tend to broaden into developments with social and long-term qualities. In contrast, the original change usually has some narrow, short-term purpose. The developer of the stirrup probably wanted to gain a quick advantage in war, but the invention led eventually to changed farming and living conditions. The inventors of the transistor wanted to improve semiconductors; they probably never dreamed their brainchild would spur nationalism in remote parts of the world.

THE NEED FOR PLANNING

Can we always foresee such spin-offs? Even if we could, can we always do much about them? The answer is no to both questions. Then why bother? Why not go along pretty much as in the past, and let come what may?

The answer lies in the fact that if we don't try to guide what we can of change we will be swamped. U.S. Electric, mentioned in the previous chapter, attempted to stop the clock, and its approach (or non-approach) to change killed it. Most of the 10,700 companies which failed in 1970 did so because of some failure in planning.

Henry B. Schacht, president of Cummins Engine Company in Indiana, expresses the anomaly this way: "In the last ten years, has our ability to plan mastered the rate of change, or has the pace of change been so swift that it has swamped our expanded ability to plan? It is my conviction that the accelerating pace of technology and change has reached a rate that has completely swamped our ability to plan. This is not to be taken, however, as an argument against planning. Planning has taken on ever-increasing importance in any organization . . . and we are obliged to use every technique at our fingertips. However, we had better recognize in that plan the unforeseen event, the unseen change, the swift and sudden ability of consumers to change their buying habits or their voting habits. Major uncertainty must be recognized in planning activities. This means that institutions no longer have the ability to plan for a period of 'nonchange'; any plan must now assume dramatic unforeseen change."

Schacht adds that this situation means that an industrial company is faced with the fact that its future depends "not on its particular technical ability, not on its particular current cost structure, or even on its particular current location or product. It means that it is solely in the hands of its people."

If you agree that the pace of change is accelerating and that this pace is overwhelming the company's ability to plan, then you are also inexorably forced to accept that your key operating mode will be flexibility.

Any organization's key assets are people and knowledge. People can be the most flexible of all assets; knowledge is the one thing that, in Schacht's words, "will give us insight into change and the consequences of change."

Of course, many companies say that people are their most important resource. Not all really believe it. While many companies may embrace their employees publicly, they privately spend most of their time with balance sheets and income statements.

Schacht continues, "In the future, we will have to attract and motivate people who are as flexible as the events of the times and who are not locked into a particular discipline, a particular way of thinking about something, or a particular present conclusion. The kinds of people that will populate the successful organizations of the future are those who look at change as a creative, thought-provoking, dynamic way of life."

That we cannot plan for everything is no reason why we cannot plan for what is within our jurisdiction. Most of the remainder of this book will detail how you can do this. But in this and the next two chapters will come some general guidelines on preparing for change, essential to grasp before specifics will grow clear.

NEW ATTITUDES TOWARD CHANGE

Your first guideline lies in a changing of your attitude toward change.

Alvin Toffler says in *Future Shock,* "Management of change is the effort to convert certain possibles into probables, in pursuit of agreed on preferables. Determining the probables calls for a science of futurism. Delineating the possible calls for an art of futurism. Defining the preferable calls for a politics of futurism."

A few groups have sprung up to study change and the future —Institute for the Future, Commission on the Year 2000, the Harvard Program on Technology and Society. Yet as individuals we must develop a habit of mind looking toward the future, not the past.

A few colleges now offer courses in futurism and change, but in most institutes of learning the emphasis remains on the past. As individuals, too, we have been programmed by our education and training to look to the past. Most of us are so unused to the habit of future-thinking that we shy away from it. While we could overestimate our ability to forecast the future, the more real danger is that we will underutilize such abilities. We must do more than anticipate probable futures. We must also widen our conception of possible futures. This requires the imagination of art.

Wild? Yet look at how science-fiction writers have predicted the future with such uncanny accuracy in regard to the moon landings.

Let's not be afraid to forecast the future. We will manage change better when we have improved forecasts of future events which become more accurate by successive approximation.

FORECASTING BUSINESS ODDS

The second general guideline involves knowing what or whether to change. Forecasting business odds on one action or another is an activity as old as business itself. This isn't the place to go deeply into such a vast subject, except to point out that the computer has greatly enlarged our abilities to arrive at reasonably correct odds in limited areas.

For instance, the computer has made possible a forecasting device called an input-output (I/O) matrix.

"Its potential for broad business planning and management, including marketing, is great and generally unrecognized," according to W. H. Fisher of Battelle Memorial Institute in Columbus, Ohio. Battelle is extending the basic I/O matrix, at the current writing, out to 1980 and 1985.

The I/O technique predicts changes in industry resulting from changing technology or customer demands, and traces shock waves of economic change as they pass through the economy. It can be used to simulate what effect any changes in technology, competition, or administration in an industry will have on individual companies.

Briefly, an input-output table breaks down all parts of an economy or a corporation. It then shows the effects of each part of that economy or corporation on each of the other parts. With the tables, you can:

■ Analyze industry growth.
■ Analyze growth of competing industries.

- Predict supply of raw materials and purchased parts.
- Analyze actual and potential markets.
- Guide internal product and market research.
- Forecast profitability as a function of technical trends.
- Forecast price trends of goods bought and goods sold.
- Suggest remedies if needed.
- Suggest acquisition candidates.
- Search out high-growth areas.
- Look for new product opportunities.
- Predict customer growth.
- Tick off timing for new plant and tools.

With tools like these or others, you can determine two vital things—where general change is coming and how you should or should not act.

SURVEYING THE PUBLIC IMPACT

Suppose that your I/O analysis suggests strongly that you need to plan for a new factory. At one time, you would go ahead and build the plant. It's not so simple now. Today you must factor in an estimate of the impact on the public that such a change might have. You must evaluate answers to questions such as these:

How can proposed new plants avoid polluting the environment? (Appropriations for new facilities built by many companies, for example, always include provisions for pollution control.)

What's the racial mix of the area in which the facility may be erected? (The administration of federal and many state laws require that the employment mix come close to the population mix of the area.)

If you conform to the area's mix, will you have the job skills to run the plant? (Because of population mix and technological advances, this often isn't the case.)

Are you prepared to spend time and money to train a new

work force up to required skills? (Youth, particularly, complain that some companies are unwilling to make adequate commitments. However, a company like General Electric has an annual educational budget larger than Princeton University's.)

Are you willing to discharge your responsibilities as a corporate citizen in the community where you will build your facility? (Here's another complaint of some youth and anti-business people—that businessmen ignore corporate citizenship.)

Questions such as the foregoing would scarcely have been considered as recently as twenty-five years ago. But industry today must weigh them along with the more conventional questions.

PLAN OF ACTION

If you can provide satisfactory answers to the public questions, you are next ready to proceed, in this case with a new factory. The following details should make up your plan of action:

Why build the plant?
What type and size of factory will it be?
How much will it cost?
Where will it be built?
When will it be completed?
Who will be in charge of the project?

The plan doesn't say how the factory will be built, whether by prefabrication methods or by conventional contracting. The plan only requires that a specification for action be prepared for each part of the policy statements; that specific sole responsibility be assigned for the task being done; and that progress be reported regularly.

MONITORING THE PLAN

Yet before the ink is dry, changes will occur affecting the goals, the forecast, or the plans. Every important assumption underlying the factors affecting results must be monitored frequently. Against each of the assumptions, record the actual figure or result as it becomes known, including an explanation if the result differs from expectations.

If any new trend emerges or an unexpected event occurs, then revise the forecast or existing plans. You can control the ordered change only if you know promptly the rate of progress toward the target. Part of your job with a plan of action is to set up the necessary reporting system for timely and accurate information. If you don't provide for this, you may fail to reach established goals because you didn't know you were failing to act in time.

A LOOK AT THE WEATHER

Mark Twain once said, "Everyone talks about the weather, but nobody does anything about it." Substitute the word "change" for "weather," and you will have a reasonably accurate statement about the subject of this book. But we *do* intend to do something about change. In the next two chapters, we will continue with two more general guidelines on preparing for change.

chapter three

Preparing for Change—II

In 1927 the famed Hawthorne experiment was made among employees of Western Electric Company in its Illinois plant. Several attempts at change to improve production of telephones—with more money, more light, more space—had brought no startling results. Then a Harvard group under Elton Mayo came in. They isolated a few departments, introduced no dramatic changes, but emphasized that people were participating in the experiment. Output soared. Why?

Because the previous changes had sprung from fallacious assumptions. You can't manage change successfully until you understand the fallacies and know how to avoid them. This sixth general guideline about change rates an entire chapter because fallacies about change abound. Among these many pitfalls, the following twelve fallacies stand out:

1. All people resist change.
2. Only large or momentous changes are worthwhile.
3. Only large or momentous changes need serious attention.
4. Everything is changing overnight.
5. Change means improvement.
6. Change brings hardships for some.
7. Change brings reward for the instigators.
8. Change is always unexpected.
9. No change is possible in a bureaucracy.
10. Technological change should and can be slowed.
11. Change usually comes by chance.
12. Man, infinitely adaptable, can stand any change.

Each of those dozen statements is misleading, deceptive, or false. Yet many managers believe some or all of them. Unwise actions stemming from such beliefs probably lie at the bottom of most mismanagements of change. Let's discuss each in detail.

ALL PEOPLE RESIST CHANGE

Nonsense. Some thrive on it; others do not. Your skill in managing change may hinge on your perceptions about your employees' tendencies.

Medical researchers report that man is equipped with an orientation response which gives him a neurological reaction to change. His senses quicken, his heartbeat speeds up when shifts in his work or other situations occur. He may enjoy the neurological reaction if it's moderate, or perhaps he can't endure it even in moderate doses. That's for you as the manager to determine. With people who enjoy the neurological response, you have a different problem. Like those who have acquired a taste for caviar, they want some frequently. If the work proves too humdrum, the change lovers will leave or, worse, stir up some excitement on the job. At the bottom of much factory and office horseplay lies boredom.

The orientation response also includes a psychic reaction to change. It motivated the Hawthorne employees where better working conditions and even better pay had not, to any dramatic extent. In short, they responded better to higher psychic income than to higher monetary reward. We'll leave until later in this book more detailed discussion of this factor, but now we can point out that you will err seriously if you persist in thinking all people resist change.

Such a fallacy has led to excuses for not inaugurating change, to wrong-headed preparations for change, or to wrong changes. The Hawthorne experiment particularly emphasizes this last point. While better lighting probably was desirable, it didn't prove crucial. The Mayo psychologists found that the people injected with added "psychic serum" outproduced those who were not so inoculated, even when the psychic have-nots labored in excellent lighting while the psychic haves worked in lighting so poor that they could scarcely read a newspaper by it.

ONLY LARGE OR MOMENTOUS CHANGES ARE WORTHWHILE

This may also be expressed as "Change for the sake of change is bad." Implicit in both statements is the notion that if you must agonize over a change you might as well agonize over something momentous; make the trouble worthwhile. The fallacy here lies in the fact that most changes are small. Yet in the aggregate they may add up to something significant.

Change for the sake of change may prove useful, even though such shifts usually are minor. This kind of change may serve the valuable purpose of stirring up people by getting their neurological and psychic juices flowing.

A magazine editor had a regular policy of making modest shifts in editorial format from time to time. While he acknowledged that he was changing for the sake of change, he defended the practice as a "stimulus to readership." He added that "people need change now and then like a person needs a new suit of clothes." In effect, the editor was stimulating readers neurologically and psychically—appealing to their senses and egos.

Thousands of experiments in industrial change since Hawthorne have also demonstrated repeatedly the value of this. But the change for change's sake that omits the neurological and psychic factors in the equation is bound to fail. At best, it will do nothing. At worst, it can demoralize employees.

It can leave buyers cold, too. For example, auto model changes that are mere face-liftings have met with less and less favor with the public in recent years. Yet changes providing some sort of neurological and psychic appeals have brought enthusiastic reaction. Ford's ill-fated Edsel failed because it was just another entry in a model range already well populated. By appealing to the buyer's eye, personal needs, or pocketbook, Ford's Mustang, Maverick, and Pinto have become textbook successes. Those three cars have stirred the buyers' juices, even though there were already other competitive entries to choose from.

Packaging experts say that a mere change in design may bring modestly good results, at best. But a change that brings even a slight touch of improved utility—such as easier opening—will prove a bonanza.

ONLY LARGE OR MOMENTOUS CHANGES NEED SERIOUS ATTENTION

Not true. Most changes are small. Nevertheless, you will have to prepare for them as effectively as the big ones for several reasons:

■ The little changes serve as your proof of credibility in preparing for the big ones.

■ An accumulation of small changes poorly prepared for can lead to large problems.

■ A change which seems trivial to you may appear monumental to others.

One company moved its office hours ahead by half an hour during the summer. It noted the change in an employee newsletter, stating that the seasonal shift came "because of popular request so that employees might have more time for recreation during the warm weather." Actually, three supervisors initiated the request so that they could reach the golf links earlier. They had checked it out with a few colleagues and had met favorable response.

But many other people objected. It conflicted with their transportation and domestic arrangements. The uproar grew so loud that management had to rescind the seemingly minor change.

Because it thought the shift in hours unimportant, management failed to prepare for it adequately. It reserved its concentrated efforts for more important matters. Yet the mistake went beyond the embarrassment of having to renege on a decision. It cost management even more seriously in lost credibility.

EVERYTHING IS CHANGING OVERNIGHT

Although change is coming faster, it is still not instantaneous. Copernicus devoted his entire adult life to changing then-prevailing notions about the sun and planetary motions. Darwin spent forty-four years in corroborating, explaining, and selling his change-generating theory of evolution by natural selection. Sir Lawrence Bragg shared a Nobel prize with his father for their joint work on analyzing crystal structures by means of x-rays—an enterprise in changing knowledge that took two lifetimes.

While city life changes, rural life continues at a slower pace. People who change frequently in one area—jobs, for example—may be stable in another, such as family relationships.

People who lament too much about the speed of change are the hand wringers. The danger here lies in the possibility that the hand wringing will leave no time or energy for positive preparation for change.

CHANGE MEANS IMPROVEMENT

This is not automatically true. What is correct is the statement made by President Nixon in his State of the Union message in 1971: "Without change there can be no progress." The test is to select the type of change that will most likely lead to progress.

The wrong changes can mean regression. For instance, Sigmund Freud, the founder of psychoanalysis, also bears responsibility for helping to introduce the habit-forming drug cocaine. He saw it as a cure for neurasthenia, did not initially recognize its addictive properties, and fatefully published a paper about it, which he himself described as "a song of praise to this magical substance."

The company that tried to adjust summer office hours thought it had introduced an improvement. It had introduced trouble instead.

To support all change enthusiastically is naïve. To support potentially productive change enthusiastically is wise.

CHANGE BRINGS HARDSHIPS FOR SOME

It need not. "Change is hard," as President Nixon also said in his 1971 State of the Union message, but it need not mean hardship.

To accept the fallacy of universal hardship, as the hand wringers do, would be to stop most productive change. If you had stopped the industrial revolution (which would probably have been impossible), you would have probably avoided the exploitation of workers, especially women and children, but you would have kept the hardships of the farm life that demeaned or enslaved the bulk of the population before the industrial revolution.

Change is always hard, but productive change lessens, not increases, hardship.

CHANGE BRINGS REWARDS
FOR THE INSTIGATORS

Unfortunately, this isn't always true, at least in the sense of reward in recognition or money. Robert Mayer, codiscoverer of the principle of the conservation of energy, was driven out of his mind by lack of recognition for his work. Ignaz Semmelweiss, who in 1847 discovered that surgeons themselves infected patients with childbed fever, also went insane. His reward was to be hounded out of Vienna by the medical profession, who resented the suggestion that they might be carrying death on their hands. He went to Budapest, made little headway with his doctrine there, and died in a mental hospital.

In short, innovation often brings conflict—with upholders of the status quo, with jealous colleagues, or with those who claim they thought of the idea first. Elias Howe received a patent for the sewing machine in 1846, but his rights to the device weren't established for another eight years, after much bitter litigation.

An inspector in an assembly plant suggested an automatic inspection device that changed him right out of a job. His employer found him another where he could—and was expected to —continue his activities for change. Some people would have said, "They don't pay me enough to make this kind of trouble for myself." Yet the inspector and others like him persist in their drive for change. No one knows exactly what motivates an innovator. Fortunately, most derive some form of psychic income from change, because they often win little else.

The cynic may inhibit the acceptance of change by intimating that the innovator merely seeks his own personal material gain.

CHANGE IS ALWAYS UNEXPECTED

This is not true. Most literate, reasonably intelligent people know, in general, that change is coming.

The danger in this fallacy lies in the assumption derived from it that the manager is absolved from the responsibility to inform people about future specific changes. On the contrary, he must avoid surprising people with specific changes. Even if an employee likes change, he probably dislikes surprises. Later we'll have more to say about communicating change. Now we can say categorically: If you have surprised someone with a change, you have failed to prepare for it.

NO CHANGE IS POSSIBLE
IN A BUREAUCRACY

It's more difficult to accomplish there, but it's still possible. To fail to attempt to change merely because you must work within a bureaucratic framework is to admit you're defeated without a fight.

One of the most celebrated examples in history of changes within a bureaucracy is Great Britain after her loss of the American colonies. One would have expected, after such a defeat, that the British Empire would have perished in the early nineteenth century. On the contrary, the nineteenth century was Britain's and its empire's golden age, thanks to thoroughgoing reform in laws, administration, and concept.

And large companies are changing, too. In a recent thirty-six-month period, 66 of 100 major American corporations announced significant organizational shake-ups. A substantial restructuring every two years in large companies is now probably average.

When General Electric provided in 1970 for a new corporate executive staff, Chairman Fred J. Borch explained it this way: "There will be a much heavier focus on forward planning—not only at the corporate level, but at the individual business level as well. I can't overstress the need for this type of planning throughout the corporation to position it for the opportunities we see ahead. . . .

"We will continue to move forward in the further decentralization of authority to the managers of the various businesses. We want to cut down on the number of decisions which are now made at the corporate executive office and board of directors levels and push these down the line to the business managers. This will be a key factor as we move ahead."

TECHNOLOGICAL CHANGE
SHOULD AND CAN BE SLOWED

History suggests that technology cannot be stopped even if it were desirable to do so. French and Belgian peasants threw their wooden shoes (*sabots,* hence the word saboteur) into textile machinery which threatened their handicraft way of life. Ned Ludd and his fellow Luddites also attempted to stop technology's clock from ticking in England. None succeeded then; none are likely to succeed now.

However, technology today is by and large uncontrolled. And there's a growing body of opinion that more control should be exercised. The rest of this book will concern itself with how these controls may be enacted—not only on technology, but on the side effects that proliferate from technology. We are not proposing how government control such change. We are suggesting how you can control those factors subject to change which come within your purview.

We don't suffer from a lack of governmental planning—far from it. In a city like New York reeling from near-disaster to near-disaster, a superabundance of planning and earnest effort has surfaced. The trouble is that the plans and efforts cancel each other out.

The problem when the technology fallacy and its related one about planning becomes accepted is that constructive change tends to get sidetracked. The issue is not that we have too much technology. It's that we don't have enough constructive and directed technology.

CHANGE COMES BY CHANCE

Only rarely does this prove true—as the result of an accident or of "serendipity"—a word coined by Horace Walpole in 1754 to denote the faculty of happening upon or making fortunate discoveries when not in search of them. While trying to develop a new type of carbon paper, National Cash Register researchers happened upon a microscopic encapsulating process that today has changed photography, medicine, and electronics. Charles Goodyear accidentally discovered the process of vulcanizing rubber. In both cases of serendipity, the researchers were hunting—but not for what they found. Goodyear sought a method to make rubber usable at all temperatures. He happened upon the vulcanizing method, but the point is that he had for years been on the alert for an answer. So, serendipity often proves to be more than blind chance. The beneficiaries of serendipity show themselves as people alert for change.

The miracle of change never comes solely by chance. On occasion, you may have observed something that becomes the germ of an idea. On a mundane level, for example, you may have grown exasperated at the way your secretary can never find anything quickly in the files. You mention the nagging problem to your wife at home.

"You need a filing system like the one I use in keeping track of recipes," your wife remarks. "File by categories, with alphabetizing within each category. I don't file the recipe for apple pie under A; I put it under P for pies. Simple, really."

And so it is. You speedily create a new filing system, borrowing the category idea from your wife. But was this chance? Only to the extent that you were looking for a new filing system. The chance occurred when your wife described her system. But eventually you would have found the trigger because you were looking for it.

The chance fallacy proves harmful when you never look for anything specific to change. Never will you find anything specific in that case, just vague observations that never pop into place in your mind to solve the problem that aches for a fresh, change-laden solution.

MAN, INFINITELY ADAPTABLE, CAN STAND ANY CHANGE

Measurable parameters limit the change that a man can absorb. Repeated stimulation of change can be physically damaging. Like a rubber band stretched too often, people lose their snap or —like a rubber band stretched too far—they break.

Psychological overstimulation is serious. Soldiers in prolonged combat conditions and victims of disaster have displayed these symptoms:

- Irritability and irascability
- Confusion and bewilderment
- Deadly apathy

Psychological overstimulation can harm a man's ability to perceive and to think and to decide. Sufferers may deny that change is taking place, or specialize in a steadily narrowing field, or revert to obsolete panaceas, or become supersimplifiers who see one formula as the answer to all problems.

We'll return to this fallacy several more times in this book. Particularly, we must exorcise this delusion if we can use creatively the seventh general guideline in preparing for change, discussed in the next chapter.

chapter four

Planning for Change—III

These office work rules were issued in 1852 and were found in the ruins of a demolished factory in Scotland:

All employees must abide by the following regulations:

1. This firm has reduced the hours of work and the clerical staff will now only have to be present between the hours of 7 A.M. and 6 P.M.

2. Daily prayers will be held each morning in the main office. The clerical staff will be present.

3. Clothing must be of a sober nature. The clerical staff will not disport themselves in raiment of bright colors.

4. A stove is provided for the benefit of the clerical staff. Coal and wood must be kept in the locker. It is recommended that each member of the clerical staff bring four pounds of coal each day during cold weather.

5. No member of the clerical staff may leave the room without

permission from Mr. Rogers. The calls of nature are permitted and clerical staff may use the garden below the second gate. This area must be kept in good order.

6. No talking is allowed during business hours.

7. The craving of tobacco, wines, and spirits is a human weakness and as such is forbidden to all members of the clerical staff.

8. Now that the hours of business have been drastically reduced, the partaking of food is allowed between 11:30 A.M. and noon, but work will not on any account cease.

The owners recognize the generosity of the new Labour Laws, but will expect a great rise in output of work in compensation for these near Utopian conditions.

We need not belabor the extent of the work rule changes in the 120 years that have passed since 1852. Yet we do need to point out the synergistic effects of change—the seventh general guideline to keep in mind in your planning for change.

In our introduction to the guidelines in Chapter 2, we compared the spin-off results of the invention of the stirrup and the transistor. The synergistic guideline has a touch of this, although it differs, largely in time span. Even some of the spin-off results of the transistor have taken twenty-five years to evolve. The stirrup's spin-offs took centuries.

Scientists have come to regard the world's weather as an interrelating system. A development in Asia eventually affects a weather development in America. Look upon the synergism of change as interrelating in an analogous way. One change bounces off another to produce still another. The interaction of the changes comes quickly, almost tumbling upon each other—a psychological shift influencing a social one, which in turn may lead to still another technological development.

The first six guidelines ask you to deal with change as if each one is separate from all others. Although such a stance is a fiction because of synergism, it is pragmatic to deal with change in this manner as much as possible. Otherwise you would be like a juggler with too many balls in the air. Yet, the time comes when you must take synergism into account.

SYNERGISM BENEATH THE SURFACE

For example, there's more to the quaint work rules of 1852 than may first meet the eye. A factory in mid-nineteenth-century Britain was a bawdy, rough-and-tumble place. The women and girls who were beginning to work there were from farms and the lower social strata of the towns and cities. By extension, some of this reputation spilled over into the office. "Nice" girls didn't work there, but employers needed females a cut above the factory types to train for the more intellectually demanding office jobs.

The canny Scottish employers of 1852 may have colored the sanctimonious tone of their work rules as an indirect "help wanted" ad—a bid to girls of the middle classes to work in an atmosphere of high decorum, including prayers, somber clothes, no drinking or smoking, and "Utopian" working hours.

Women weren't paid as much as men for the same work in those days, and the employer probably was looking for a way to offset the expense of shorter hours. But this also coincided with the early stirring of women's emancipation in mid-nineteenth-century Britain.

It's no accident, either, that a flood of new office machines was just arriving at this time. The first calculating machine was introduced in England in 1823. A rudimentary typewriter saw service as early as 1850. So, in the Scottish work rules of 1852, we can see synergism at work—changing laws, social customs, economic needs, even technology, all interrelating.

WHEN SYNERGISM CANCELS OUT

Sometimes the synergism of change can cause a virtual paralysis. For example, consider the case of Consolidated Edison Company of New York. This privately owned utility provides electricity, gas, and steam to some 9 million people in metropolitan New

York and Westchester County. It is vital to that heavily populated area:

- It sells $70 million worth of electricity a year to the city of New York alone.
- It pays the city about $140 million a year in taxes.
- It spends an average of $250 million a year on construction in the city, providing 20 per cent of the employment in the building trades in New York.
- It is the second-largest employer in the metropolitan area.

However, it has the lowest rate of return of any private utility in America. It is plagued with power shortages, high rates, customer complaints, and continued wrangling with government officials. It may have to ration electricity for some years into the future.

Mismanagement? No. "The company is headed by exceptionally intelligent and competent managers," says George Cabot Lodge, associate professor of business administration at the Harvard Business School. "Instead, this problem and the other pressing problems of the company derive from the political structures that surround it and the tension, confusion, and competition of interests they embody."

SYNERGISM ON THE PLUS SIDE

On the other hand, the synergism of change sometimes has a favorable result. Among the many industries that have grown greatly in the past forty-five years are aircraft, commercial aviation, natural gas, plastics, electronics, plywood, aluminum, pleasure boats, road building, air conditioning, frozen foods, and various industries producing durable consumer goods.

The growing number of industries tends to dampen the effects of any favorable or unfavorable developments upon the economy because such developments affect different industries in different degrees and at different times. As a case in point, take inventory adjustments. Inevitably, some industries allow their inventories to become too large or too small relative to sales. In an economy of a few industries, the efforts to remedy such errors may disturb the whole economy. The greater the number of industries, the less disturbing to the whole economy will be the attempts of some industries to restore the best ratio between inventories and sales. For instance, the General Motors strike in late 1970 undoubtedly dampened the economy, but not as seriously as one would fear.

The foregoing examples of negative and positive results from synergism may be termed passive and unplanned in the sense that they lead to an effect that was not anticipated and cannot be readily controlled. There's also an active, unplanned kind of synergism—for instance, growing competitiveness that can be controlled, at least to a degree.

One reason for keener competition is the growing competition between old goods and new goods. This sort of change grows more important because people are becoming better supplied with goods and can easily postpone buying the new. Thus the amount of durable consumer goods owned per person, expressed in constant dollars, nearly tripled between 1900 and 1970.

Another reason why competition grows keener is industry's greater capacity to improve products and methods. Every enterprise is threatened increasingly with the possibility that its rival will bring out a new and better product. So, the rivalry accelerates to find the new and different.

This new competition may come from another industry as more and more discoveries turn up more and more products, materials, and processes. General Electric, as a case in point, operates in fifteen of the twenty-two standard industrial classifications. The only protection is to step up your own research and development, leading to still more competition—a snowball effect.

Finally, competition is being stimulated by the growing rewards for successful innovation. The bigger the market, the greater the rewards reaped by the developers of the new product.

And never have the rewards been greater than in the American market, which accounts for 40 per cent of the world's total consumption.

This is why the drive for change is the greatest in the United States—because the rewards are the greatest.

USING UNPLANNED
SYNERGISM TO ADVANTAGE

What can we do about the unplanned synergisms? Anticipate them. Plan for them as you would plan for a storm or fair weather. Plant and plan your crops to take the best advantage of what you think will be that weather of change.

Example: The synergism of change has led to a service- and recreation-oriented society. In late 1970, General Electric Company startled the business world by announcing it was launching a new subsidiary to produce movies, television shows, documentaries, and perhaps even stage shows. This electrical equipment manufacturer, which also produces jet engines, plastics, industrial diamonds, defense gear, and thousands of other products, is taking advantage of synergism which it had never planned.

ACTIVELY PLANNED SYNERGISM

But can you go one step even further and plan a change with still another desirable change in mind? The answer is yes, and this is the area where the most dramatic and rewarding changes may occur. What follows are two examples—one in the psychological area and the other in the technological.

In 1960, Douglas MacGregor, a professor of industrial relations at Massachusetts Institute of Technology, wrote *The Human Side of Enterprise.* He contended that most managements the world over, regardless of political orientation, base their strategies on the false assumption (theory X) that man is lazy, shuns work, wants no responsibility, and reports for duty only to avoid the punishment of material deprivation.

He acknowledged that theory X worked, by and large, but he said there was something better, which he called theory Y. He turned to the theories of Abraham Maslow of Brandeis University, one of the mavericks of American psychology, for broader concepts. Earlier Maslow had published *Motivation and Personality,* in which he listed human needs. Most fundamental came the physiological, then in ascending order came security, love or a sense of belonging, reputation or self-esteem, and finally, when others had been satisfied, the demand for self-actualization—for a man "to be actualized in what he is potentially."

The late Dr. MacGregor wove these concepts into a new management and motivation theory. Who would ever actually use them when theory X had worked time and time again? A number of managers have tried it, often with dramatic results.

One is Arthur H. Kuriloff. He had too many defective instruments coming off the assembly line. He adopted theory Y, reorganizing management to delegate authority down the ranks. Time clocks disappeared. The workers on the assembly line, who formerly had learned and performed small tasks, were reorganized into teams of seven, each team responsible for producing a complete instrument, with distribution of tasks left to mutual agreement. At first confusion reigned, but the more skilled eventually taught the less, the helpless learned from the ingenious. After a little more than two years, Kuriloff could report in his book *Reality in Management* that man-hour productivity had increased by 30 per cent while reports by customers of defective instruments had decreased by 70 per cent. Absenteeism fell to half the local average.

Could this happen only in America? Not at all. Willem James made even more spectacular use of theory Y at an oil refinery in Rotterdam, Holland. He refined 80,000 barrels of crude oil a day in 1965. He was dissatisfied with efficiency and profits. He concluded that a philosophical reorganization was necessary. While theory Y was not entirely applicable to a refinery, he made adaptations. He replaced the hourly wage with a monthly salary. He discontinued former checks on employees reporting ill except to make sure that they were well when they returned. Wherever possible, groups were formed within departments and assigned an objective, but placed on their own as to the means of accomplishment. Advice was available, but management functioned more as consultant than boss. The group had to produce. It all added up to a "management by objective" theme.

"Job enrichment" was probably one of the more critical reforms because as soon as man had mastered a task he was urged to learn another. The more he could do, the more money he made. Yet this didn't appear to be the ultimate reward. Adventure, challenge, the right to dare were introduced into the life of the industrial worker.

Results: Manpower was cut by 49 per cent, productivity per man increased by 172 per cent. Labor turnover decreased from 10 per cent to 2 per cent, lending weight to James' statement, "We have a happy oil refinery."

Robert Ardrey in *The Social Contract* writes: [1] "In our search for hypotheses of predictive value, I suggest that the concept of human organization motivated by material need has been sufficiently successful to destroy itself; and that if we do not enlarge our concepts of innate human need—our portrait of the human being himself—then our societies will eventually either lapse into apathy or explode into anarchy."

Another kind of actively planned synergism lies in technology. Technological change and expansion bring into existence the kind of skills, resources and institutions which further growth of productivity requires. They create staffs of scientists and engineers to make technological innovations; capital-goods industries to make the equipment a changing technology requires; research labs in private industry and research firms that undertake re-

[1] Permission to reprint granted by Atheneum Publishers, New York.

search work on contract; and all kinds of related institutions that facilitate growth, such as appropriate developments in the capital markets and new forms of securities and new loan arrangements to meet special problems. The new developments include financial technicians who are skilled at inventing the new kind of financial arrangements needed to finance growth under various conditions.

Technological change and expansion create large vested interests in further technological changes and in further expansion. Technological change brings into existence an increasing number of enterprises that depend for their markets upon the rate at which technology changes and the rate at which industry buys new plant and equipment. These enterprises do not let the rate of technological change occur at whatever rate independent engineers and scientists happen to make discoveries, and they do not let the rate at which equipment is bought depend upon the rate at which users of equipment see fit to purchase it. The firms whose markets depend upon technological change and the expansion of industry attempt to accelerate the rate of innovation by hiring scientists and engineers to make discoveries and by offering users of equipment new machines that they must buy in order to remain competitive.

This is a fundamental and planned active change in the nature of our economy. During most of the history of the world, the rate of technological change was mostly unplanned accident. Economic calculus was not applied to it. Today in the United States we have a large and rapidly growing new industry that the late Sumner Slichter, a Harvard professor, called "the industry of discovery."

Its product is knowledge. The industry consists of the various laboratories and organizations that depend upon discovery for their living and that are interested in making money by speeding the rate of discovery.

The industry of discovery employs triple the number of research scientists and engineers that it did thirty years ago. It promises to grow even more because its size appears limited only by the availability of suitable people.

Now that we have looked at seven general guidelines in preparing for change, we are ready to get down to specifics. Of course, changes of various sorts go on all the time—some simultaneously. But it's easier to understand and study change if we look at each general type separately. In this book, we will look at four general types—in technology, methods, organization, and people. First, we'll consider the specifics of that basic engine of change, technology.

part two

Technologies Change

chapter five

The Nature of Technological Change

The dictionary defines *technology* as "the sum of the ways in which a social group provide themselves with the material objects of their civilization."

To understand technological change, keep this definition in mind as we trace a little history of some significant shifts in the past. The myths have it that James Watt sat dreaming as a boy in front of a boiling kettle. Later, he translated that image of the kettle into the steam engine. Or one day Thomas Edison awakened from one of his cat naps with an idea for a filament that at last made the electric lamp a practical reality.

These pretty stories ignore the context in which two highly significant inventions were made and accordingly obscure the nature of technological change.

THE STEAM ENGINE

The facts of the steam engine are that Watt belonged to a closely linked group of "applied scientists," as they would now be called, in the Universities of Glasgow and Edinburgh. This also included Joseph Black, whose discovery of latent heat lay at the bottom of Watt's improvements to the Newcomen engine. John Roebuck, an industrialist and another member of the group, financed many of his early efforts. These men passed ideas back and forth. They were dissatisfied with the grossly inefficient Newcomen engine, and they saw the practical need for an engine that could pump water out of mines and move it in canals and harbors.

In this context slowly emerged Watt's steam engine in the eighteenth century, growing out of previous discoveries, helped by other contemporary ideas, and filling a pragmatic need. The uses of the engine multiplied beyond the water-pumping application, but slowly. Although Watt's first patent was issued in 1769, the first practical use on a railroad didn't occur until 1801. This is despite the fact that Sir Isaac Newton had predicted steam-propelled rail carriages as early as 1680.

THE ELECTRIC LAMP

Nor did the electric lamp burst on the scene without antecedents and contemporary relatives.

During the mid-nineteenth century, the electrical industry was established on the basis, largely, of supplying telegraph services. Significantly, Edison's early career began as a telegraph operator. Electric motors for tramways and stationary machinery had also been developed, leading to much expansion. By 1880, a keenly competitive electrical industry flourished in the United States, Britain, Germany, and France, especially. Yet middle-aged men in it were well aware when it had scarcely not existed and knew that new applications and design improvements followed each other extremely rapidly.

However, one development about to revolutionize the industry still more sprang from outsiders. Joseph Wilson Swan, an English chemist, made experimental incandescent lamps ir' 1860 using a high-resistance conductor, carbonized paper, as a filament. Swan's experiments brought no commercial fruit, partly because his interests lay more in the photographic area and in the chemical aspects of his various activities.

It's not known for certain if Edison was aware of Swan's experiments. In any event, it happens again and again that two or more people or groups work independently on the same idea at or nearly the same time, without either being aware of the other's work.

In 1922 the Columbia sociologist William Fielding Ogburn in his book *Social Change* cited 148 cases of major discoveries made independently by two or more investigators. The fact that there was nearly simultaneous discovery in everything from thermodynamics, chemistry, and mathematics to sewing machines, reapers, and airplanes illustrates that innovators everywhere are quick to sense what AT&T's Henry M. Boettinger calls "economic friction points." The director of management services for American Telephone & Telegraph Company characterizes the technologist "as a sort of Machiavellian opportunist, patrolling and probing an army's defenses. When he anticipates or spots a hole, the technologist rushes to his workshop and invents a weapon that will plug the defense gap . . . economic friction point."

While it's true that lags may exist between these discoveries, such lags usually can be measured in months or a year or two. Even the Swan-Edison case of a nineteen-year lag indicates that nobody has ever really invented anything entirely alone.

Edison, who always quickly sensed economic friction points, saw the electric lamp as an ideal consumer for the burgeoning power-generating industry. He probably did waken from a cat nap with the idea of carbonized cotton thread as the filament material. But he had already spent more than $40,000 in fruitless experiments on the lamp. This idea worked after hundreds of others had failed.

When Edison had his patent on the lamp in 1879, he tried to sell the idea to some of the electrical companies already in business. No luck. Edison was bumping into a phenomenon common in technology—people already in the field are slow to accept new ideas, especially from outsiders. Alexander Graham Bell couldn't sell his idea of the telephone to the telegraph companies and founded AT&T to promote his invention. Other "outsider" examples abound: General Electric Company researchers invented Man-Made diamonds. Bell Telephone Laboratory people developed a type of transistor.

HISTORY'S LESSONS
ABOUT TECHNOLOGY

These foregoing, brief sketches about two technological changes tell us several things about the phenomenon.

Donald Schon, president of the Organization for Social and Technical Innovation, writes in *Technology and Change* [1] that there are three historical stages. First comes the craft stage where technology is the property of a few individuals. "There are no general principles, no explanations of phenomena; only observations of what happens when you do this or that," he says. "Today there are still islands of craft in papermaking, textiles, leather, graphic arts, ceramics; whole companies are dependent on the real or imagined skill of a few men."

In the craft phase, most of the communication among people with similar interests is face to face, by personal letters and by other small-scale contact of a peculiarly intimate and undisturbed type. This prevailed in Watts' day. The little coteries and

[1] Reprinted by permission of the publisher, Delacorte Press, Dell Publishing Co., Inc., New York.

provincial societies spread the word about technological developments. But from about 1850 on, a giant foot pressed on the accelerator of technological change in the appearance of scientific journalism.

In 1800 there were less than ten scientific journals published in the British Isles. By 1900 there were more than 130. The years from 1800 to 1825 saw the appearance of new general scientific journals, but their numbers are fairly constant (about 15) from 1830 onwards. From 1825, the main growth is in specialized and technical journals; there were three in 1825 and over forty by 1860. From mid-century onwards the published transactions and journals of learned societies began to grow rapidly, from a dozen in 1850 to about seventy in 1900.

These British journals were available to the specialists in America, but this country didn't begin to publish such publications in impressive numbers until the turn of the century.

These journals helped open the ways to the second phase of technological change—as scientific analysis, engineering, and chemistry begin to replace craft. "But technology," Schon says, "is still fighting its battle against craft and is still very much a subordinate function—a service to production or sales." He points out that the auto industry is still largely in this second phase of development.

Edison had elements of the craftsmen in his method and elements of the second stage. He always yearned for commercial development of his inventions. But he never succeeded as a businessman to the extent he prevailed as an inventor-craftsman. One of his business ventures has today evolved into General Electric Company; yet he had lost any voice in its management by the time of his death in 1931.

Edison's genius was such that he had a foot into the third stage of technological change, also. This is the organized approach to discovery, including research for its own sake without a specific idea of where it will lead you.

In this third stage, according to Schon, "Technology comes

into its own. The company has extended and consolidated its scientific grasp of production and quality control. It begins to undertake research into the materials and processes related to its field without being sure of where that research will lead. Work is done toward the development of new products and processes to replace those in existence." He names the chemical industry as an outstanding example.

WHY RETARDATION?

You can understand why an industry whose existence is an outgrowth of relatively recent scientific discoveries (electronics, for instance) engages in third-phase research. But why are other industries mired in phase 2 or even phase 1?

No single factor accounts for such retardation, but the nature of its competition may provide a clue. For instance, in the United States auto industry the four companies sharing nearly 90 per cent of the market felt no strong pressure to attempt bold technological advances until it ran into an unexpected public hullaballoo over air pollution.

The government-regulated railroad industry—almost a cliché as a horrible example of neglect in research—is described by an outside technologist who has consulted with it on various problems as "doing nothing with great verve."

Jacob Goldman of Xerox, Inc., believes that companies using research well are systems-oriented rather than product-oriented. That is, they look at the entire system into which the particular product fits, rather than at the narrow segment of the product itself. "That's why a lot of new technologies didn't come from the companies where you might have expected them. Synthetic fibers came not from textile manufacturers but from the chemical industry.

"Transistors didn't come from radio people but from the telephone company. Synthetic industrial diamonds came from the electrical industry, not from the machine-tool companies."

He calls this the "buggy-whip syndrome" because the buggy-whip makers never planned for the obsolescence of their chief product. "They should have thought of themselves as accelerator companies, and then perhaps they could have survived and made the transition to automobiles and the airplane age." He says the great innovators of society today are "companies like AT&T which thinks of itself as being in the communications business and not the telephone business, and IBM, which sees itself as in the information-services business and not in the manufacture of computers."

A SECOND DIMENSION

Thus one vital aspect of technological change is context: it grows out of other discoveries, their communication, and economic developments which eventually come together to give birth to a needed change. They may come from a genius, but not a lonely genius out of touch with the world around him.

In the third phase of technological change, man has organized it to increase greatly the speed at which discoveries are made—to add a second dimension to the nature of technological change. In the words of Alvin Toffler in *Future Shock,* "Acceleration is one of the most important and least understood of all social forces."

You can gain a notion of this acceleration from a condensed account of progress in transportation. In 6000 B.C. the fastest transportation available to man over long distances was the camel caravan, averaging 8 miles per hour. The chariot, developed about 1600 B.C., proved a significant development because it raised maximum speed to about 20 miles per hour. For nearly 3,500 years it retained the speed crown. Even the first mail coach in England in 1784 averaged a mere 10 miles per hour. The early steam locomotives huffed and puffed to a top speed of 13 miles per hour. The great sailing ships of the early nineteenth century made less than half that speed. Not until the 1880s did man reach a speed of 100 miles per hour, with the help of a better steam locomotive. It took the human race millions of years to attain such a record.

Yet it took only another fifty-eight years to quadruple the limit, so that by 1938 airborne man was exceeding 400 miles per hour. That was doubled in a mere twenty years. By the 1960s, rocket planes approached speeds of 4,000 miles per hour, and men in space capsules were circling the earth at 18,000 miles per hour.

You can measure speed, distances traveled, power harnessed. The same accelerative trend appears here and in thousands of other measures. We now see a fantastic spurt forward in technology on hundreds of fronts. Why? Because technology feeds on itself. Technology makes more technology possible. First comes an idea, then its practical application, third its diffusion through society. The diffusion through society, in turn, helps generate more creative ideas. This process has operated since man left the tree tops. The evidence multiplies that the time between each step in this cycle steadily shortens.

Appollonius of Perga discovered conic sections, but the idea was not applied to engineering problems for another 2,000 years. Paracelsus discovered that ether could be used as an anesthetic, but centuries elapsed before it was used for that purpose. Even in more modern times, delays sometimes occur. In 1837 a machine that mowed, threshed, tied straw into sheaves, and poured grain into sacks was invented, based on technology already a score of years old. Yet the machine didn't go onto the market until the combine was actually marketed. The English issued a patent for a typewriter as early as 1714, but that office machine didn't come onto the market for nearly another 150 years.

Today such lags between idea and application are rare—not because we are more active or alert but because we have the communication and social devices to speed the process.

Of a score of major innovations—frozen food, antibiotics, integrated circuits, and synthetic leather—more than 60 per cent has been slashed from the average time needed for a major discovery to be transformed into a useful technological form since the beginning of this century. And our industry works to reduce that lag still more.

If the time between idea and product has been reduced, the time needed to spread the product or idea through society has also been cut, thanks largely to communication.

For the vacuum cleaner, the electric range, and the refrigerator —all introduced before 1920—the average span between introduction and saturation was about thirty-four years. Yet for a group introduced between 1939 and 1959—including the electric frying pan, television, and the washer-dryer combination—the span was only eight years.

If technology is the primary engine of change, knowledge— communicated knowledge—is its fuel. And the fuel grows richer.

The rate at which man has been acquiring knowledge about himself and the universe has been spiraling upward for 10,000 years. The rate leaped upward with the invention of writing, but it was still slow. Gutenberg's invention of movable type in the fifteenth century gave a sharply accelerative thrust to the process. Before 1500, Europe produced no more than 1,000 new book titles per year. By 1950, four and a half centuries later, the rate had skyrocketed to 120,000 new titles per year in Europe alone. By 1960, just a decade later, it had jumped still more. By the mid-1960s, 1,000 new titles were appearing per day, worldwide.

Today, the number of scientific journals and articles is doubling about every fifteen years. Now the United States government alone generates 100,000 reports each year, plus 450,000 articles, books, and papers. On a worldwide basis, scientific and technical literature mounts at a rate of some 60 million pages a year.

Investigators a century ago used to scrounge for every scrap of printed information on their field of interest. Now they are deluged by written information. Philip Siekevitz, a biochemist, says, "What has been learned in the last three decades about the nature of living beings dwarfs in extent of knowledge any comparable period of scientific discovery in the history of mankind."

And it's all in writing somewhere. Fortunately the computer burst onto the scene about 1950. Toffler points out: "With its unprecedented power for analysis and dissemination of extremely varied kinds of data in unbelievable quantities and at mind-staggering speeds, it has become a major force behind the latest acceleration in knowledge acquisition. Combined with other increasingly powerful analytical tools for observing the invisible universe around us, it has raised the rate of knowledge acquisition to dumbfounding speeds."

It has also helped disseminate that knowledge with increasingly sophisticated computer searching techniques.

BY THE YEAR 2000

In the next chapters we'll have more to say about the use of such knowledge to predict future technologies. Now, let's see what one technologist, David Sarnoff, retired chairman of RCA, sees will happen by the end of this century. Here's what he sees will happen as "science and technology advance more (by 2000) than in all the millenia since man's creation."

Food. "The Western nations by the turn of the century will be able to produce twice as much food as they consume, and if political conditions permit advanced food production and conservation techniques could be extended to the overpopulated and undernourished areas."

Raw Materials. "Technology will find ways of replenishing or replacing the world's industrial materials. The ocean depths will be mined for nickel, cobalt, copper, manganese, and other vital ores. Chemistry will create further substitutes for existing materials, transmute others into new forms and substances, and find hitherto unsuspected uses for the nearly 2,000 recognized minerals that lie within the earth's surface."

Energy. "The energy at man's disposal is potentially without limit. One pound of fissionable uranium the size of a golf ball has the potential energy of nearly 1,500 tons of coal, and the supply of nuclear resources is greater than all the reserves of coal, oil, and gas. Increasingly, electric power plants will be nuclear, and atomic energy will be a major power source, particularly in the underdeveloped areas."

Health. "Science will find increasingly effective ways of deferring death. In this country, technology will advance average life expectancy from the Biblical three score and ten toward the five-score mark, and it will be a healthier, more vigorous, and more useful existence. The electron has become the wonder weapon of the assault on disease and disability. Ultraminiature electronic devices implanted in the body will regulate human organs whose functions have become impaired."

Genetics. "Before the century ends . . . science will unravel the genetic code which determines the characteristics that pass from parent to child. Science will also take an inanimate grouping of simple chemicals and breathe into it the spark of elementary life, growth, and reproduction. . . . New and healthier strains of plants and animals will be developed."

Communications. "Through communication satellites, laser beams, and ultraminiaturization, it will be possible by the end of the century to communicate with anyone, anywhere, at any time, by voice, sight, or written message."

Travel. "From techniques developed for lunar travel and other purposes, new forms of terrestrial transport will emerge. Earth vehicles riding on air cushions and powered by nuclear energy or fuel cells will traverse any terrain and skim across water."

Defense. "In tomorrow's national command post, the country's civilian and military leaders will see displayed on a cycloramic color television screen a continuously changing, instantly updated computer synthesis of pertinent events around the world. . . . The computer will report, in written form, what and where the problems are. Another section will delineate the alternatives, and suggest appropriate actions, and still another will assess the probable and actual results. But in all cases, final decisions will be matters for human judgment."

Air and Space. "Around earth a network of weather satellites will predict with increasing accuracy next season's floods and droughts, extremes of heat and cold. It will note the beginnings of typhoons, tornadoes, and hurricanes in time for the disturbances to be diverted or dissipated before they reach dangerous intensity. Ultimately, the development of worldwide, long-range meteorological theory may lead to the control of weather and climate. Space will become hospitable to sustained human habitation."

Those predictions were published by *Fortune* in May 1964. They have stood up well thus far, in contrast to other technological prognostications.

Some people would argue that so many technological forecasts have turned out badly that the entire practice of predicting is now suspect. Far from it. Forecasting—with as much accuracy as possible, of course—is essential. In the next two chapters we will show how good predictions lie at the bottom of preparing for and influencing the effects of technological change.

chapter six

Preparing for Technological Change

We live in the midst of a paradox. At the time when technological change threatens to overwhelm us with its volume, complexity and speed, some among us attempt to deny or denigrate its importance to our society.

In a recent nationwide survey, 34 per cent of the adults surveyed believe that at least some of the technical progress made by large companies does more to worsen the quality of life than to improve it. Among students, 41 per cent of those from disturbed campuses and 37 per cent from others held negative opinions about the value of technology.

Glenn T. Seaborg, former Atomic Energy Commission chairman and president in 1972 of the American Association for the Advancement of Science, believes, "We must try to reverse the disillusionment with science of the American public. And we're going to have to make science more relevant to human problems than we have in the past."

Economist Anthony Wiener, chairman of the Hudson Institute's Research Management Council, says: "U.S. science is not in apocalyptic trouble. But it's in a very painful period of having to change the way it does things."

The disparagement of technology is not new. The two most influential economic theorists of this century, Alfred Marshall and John Maynard Keynes, both excluded technical change in their models of the modern economic system. This comes despite the fact that the United States, parts of Asia, and most of Western Europe have experienced extraordinary growth in the past quarter century largely because of advancements in scientific knowledge. Some 90 per cent of all the scientists who ever lived are alive today. More medical research has been done since World War II than in all previous years. Half of the chemical industry's 1975 sales revenues are expected to come from products now in the introductory stages or not even invented yet.

Nevertheless, some otherwise intelligent managers make statements such as, "We have more technology than we know what to do with." Or, "If we could turn off these lab and science guys for about five years, we'd all be better off."

Most managers, however, know better. Even people who make such statements are probably just letting off steam. Most know that corporate and government health depends on managers' ability to anticipate technological changes and to shape the change to the operation's advantage or the operation to the change.

Many nontechnical people also have become uneasily aware that technology has assumed transcendent importance. They reluctantly agree with statements such as this by Dr. A. V. Feigenbaum, president of General Systems Company, Inc.: "Some of the new technological systems are so powerful they go to the very roots of the way you manage things, and unless this technology is understood, you lose control. Technology, in fact, has become so powerful it can't be left to the technologists."

When you come to that conclusion, the nontechnical manager (to whom this and the next chapter are largely addressed) must take two basic steps to prepare for technological change. First, you must learn about technology itself. Second, you must learn to manage it even though you are not a technologist.

LEARNING ABOUT TECHNOLOGY

Do most nontechnical people welcome the opportunity to control and foster technology? Not many. At heart, some fear the responsibility. In self defense, they take a conservative, often isolationist stance in the midst of a deluge of technological advances. How, then, can the generalist manager make himself more at ease in a difficult area? Among the many actions you can take, the following five stand out:

1. Have courage

"I think we are in constant danger—not from technology, but from losing our nerve," says Dr. Herbert A. Simon, professor of computer science and psychology and associate dean of Carnegie-Mellon University's Graduate School of Industrial Administration. He explains his thesis: "When Columbus came to this continent, he could come in hope of fulfilling his own goals—and in ignorance of the plague and syphilis that he was bringing the Indians. We don't have that ignorance anymore. We know a lot about the germs we are bringing with us, and we tend to become overawed by the responsibility for these waves of consequences of any action that we take."

Dr. Simon made that statement at a symposium sponsored by the National Industrial Conference Board on "How to Survive Technology," a title implying that technology itself has elements of the plague or syphilis.

Dr. John R. Coleman, Haverford College president, commented at the same symposium that technology today is the whipping boy for questions of life and death alike—"the death technology in Vietnam, being used to play out a script of senselessness and brutality with some modicum of efficiency—and, at the other end of the spectrum, the life technology that produces more babies and prolongs the lives of more old people before we figure out how to cope with the ones we have."

In the face of such pressures, it does take courage to proceed with technology. Added to this is the fact that it takes courage to change in any way. A nontechnical manager may fear technology because:

■ It means change, uncertainty, risk over projects only partially understood.

■ It multiplies complexity, shifts power, threatens a manager's control.

■ It threatens radical rearrangements, in conflict with the inate conservatism of some managers who have a vested interest in the status quo. In the words of Dr. Lewis Branscomb, director of the National Bureau of Standards, "technology has completely changed the marketplace in ways that are frustrating to the consumer, to the business man, and to the politician."

■ It has created a new breed of men in our society, the technologists. In the words of L. D. Smullin, head of MIT's Department of Electrical Engineering, "We don't really know what to do with our fancy, sophisticated engineers and scientists in terms of the ordinary, daily needs of people."

■ It has raised profound and disturbing ethical questions. It brings us air pollution along with air conditioning, mountainous rubbish along with convenience foods.

In the face of these negatives, should you ignore technology? Of course not, if only because you cannot. Dr. Branscomb suggests that you can find new courage when you:

■ Analyze the extent to which technology is producing changes within your purview.

■ Recognize that most decisions about technology are being made by laymen and not technologists.

■ Realize that technology is no threat—it's decisions about technology that pose the threat. "Decisions about technology," he advises, "are the important phase of living with it."

You can keep your courage up, also, by reminding yourself that the risks of technology may pay off handsomely.

Consider the case of Chester Carlson's invention of xerography. A young IBM marketing man spotted the report of the patent award in *The New York Times* in 1940, tried unsuccessfully for a year and a half to interest his company in it, and finally gave up. Eastman Kodak Company even published an abstract of Carlson's first patent in its own *Patent Abstracts* in 1943. But it also failed to pursue the matter.

Finally in October 1948 the little Haloid Company (now Xerox, Inc.) showed the results of its courage when it introduced xerography and the now-famous office copying machine. Xerox, Inc., an enormously successful company now, is only one example of how technology can pay off. The building-services and cleaning-products division of Minnesota Mining and Manufacturing Company grew out of a courageous management decision to allow one researcher to work on just a single, far-out endeavor— the study of nonwoven nylon materials. He came up with Scotch-Brite—a product with so many uses that the company sees virtually no end to its growth potential.

2. Be prepared psychologically

Courage is only one aspect of the psychological shield you need in preparing yourself for technological change. Examples:

■ When originally flexible people repeatedly must defend decisions, various factors force them to become technically rigid. They soon suffer from technological stasis.

■ Many people tend to magnify the problems they face (thus enlarging their own importance). This leads to massive programs, and the bigger the program, generally, the less likely the chances for clearcut success.

■ After running a new program for a while, many involved with it tend to convince themselves that no further improvement in technology will occur soon. They then can use several devices to insure that their prognostication comes true. They may control research and development funding in such a way that progress is indeed blocked. They may assign people to the project with stand-pat attitudes. A review committee, with carefully selected members, can stultify progress.

So in learning about technology, be on guard against constantly forcing your people to justify their actions, watch out for the proliferating program, and take care that the older program does not become a victim of technological conservatism.

The present state of mind of people without technical backgrounds is analogous with that of French peasants when the metric system was introduced, points out Dr. Myron Tribus, formerly assistant secretary for science and technology of the U.S. Department of Commerce and now senior vice-president for Xerox. "Most people then didn't go to school. Cutting things in half was a natural system—numbers and fractions were easy to deal with, decimals were not. The metric system became a kind of tyranny over those who didn't know," he says.

Dr. Tribus advises that every manager periodically become a student of his technical people, taking time out to learn what they know. Just doing that will do much to establish the necessary rapport.

"There's a tremendous psychological victory to be gained this way," he says. "It is the sincerest form of flattery, of course, but it enormously increases the chance that your decisions will be based on understanding. Then when you are able to make a decision on the basis of what they say, you have raised them to the highest possible level. They feel comfortable. How unlike saying, 'Don't bother me with all those details. Just tell me how much it's going to cost and get out.' "

Dr. Branscomb adds this note about psychological preparation: "One of the criteria for living with technology is the recognition that intuition plays a key role. This means that managers, politicians, and industrialists must increase their experience with technology so that they can trust their intuition."

3. Be informed

Many managers of technological change fail because they don't understand the nature of the innovation. Rarely is a manager too stupid or too lazy to understand the technological change. The problem goes deeper than that. He may not clearly understand that he is making a technological decision. Or he may not clearly see the implications of the decision.

A magazine publisher, faced with rising costs, set his production people the task of cost improvement. They recommended type-setting by computer and a new printing method. The publisher okayed the change, but he soon discovered that the revised production methods required modifying the magazine layout, new methods of making type changes, and a longer copy-to-printing time because the new methods had less flexibility than the old. The publisher made a technological decision based on inadequate understanding of the technologies involved. He thought he was managing a cost improvement; actually he was managing an innovation.

Another difficulty often lies in stopping too soon—not digging for the complete information. This may partly explain why IBM and Eastman Kodak did not pursue Carlson's xerographic invention.

A related problem consists of too narrow a range of interests. At first thought, one would believe that industrial diamonds would not interest General Electric. But it already produced metallurgical products for cutting and shaping purposes. Industrial diamonds perform such functions. Yet GE had no source for the natural material except to buy it on the open market. It broadened its interest—eventually to result in Man-Made diamonds.

Dr. Tribus offers this to the generalist manager: "If the manager isn't technically qualified himself . . . in effect he ought to say (to the technologist), 'Look, I'm not qualified to understand this. Please explain it to me in my own terms. Why should I be doing this?' "

To inform yourself, you ask questions. This involves knowing if you are on the right track, knowing if you have the capabilities among your people to do the job. First, you have to generate a sense (intuition, again) as to whether now is a time for action. This is not a technical review, but rather sufficient discussion and perceptive questioning to attempt to understand the basic performance characteristics of what the innovators are trying to sell you, why it's better, why competitors have not pursued it, and what fundamental factors make it feasible.

Maxwell W. Hunter II, assistant to the vice president at Lockheed Missiles & Space Company's Space Systems Division, explains the reasons for asking nasty technical questions: "Engineers and scientists cannot be trusted any more than other human beings can. Sometimes they are just excited about their ideas. Sometimes they are naïve about requirements. Sometimes their viewpoint is dangerously narrow. Sometimes, of course, they are about to make their manager a hero! Sometimes, alas, they are frauds. If the answers that come back to perceptive questions are completely devoid of technical substance, one can safely assume that he is getting a technical snow job rather than useful information. . . . The only way to understand is to dig, question, remember, and dig again until the essence is understood . . . in order to ascertain whether revolutionary fervor is appropriate."

Dr. Branscomb summarizes: "I think the fundamental issue is to get managers to take time to step back once in a while and ask, 'Do I really understand the change going on around me? Do

I know how they're affecting my company? Where did this change come from?' "

4. Be realistic

An official of a firm widely admired for its innovative skill admits that "our research management is only 8 to 10 per cent of ideal." And he adds, "Others do it even worse."

You can't understand and measure technological innovation in the sense that you do marketing or other aspects of an operation. Management here requires an intuition to a degree not usually necessary elsewhere. Because intuition is notoriously imprecise, results rarely will be ideal.

Corporate spending on basic and applied research reached an estimated $3 billion in 1969. Many businessmen understandably wonder what they get for that large amount of money. More and more concerned executives grope toward better management of what *Fortune* magazine calls "this most elusive of corporate functions."

Mr. Hunter discusses just one aspect of such imprecision: "The estimation of the timing of future technical achievement is not subject to engineering or scientific analysis. Limits may be set as bounds on the problem, but precise timing is a matter of opinion, and opinions vary violently among technical people."

Many other imprecisions exist in technology—market potentials, costs to implement, competitive probabilities, and so on. The upshot is that the manager of such change must be realistic, ready to settle for less precise results than in other business functions.

5. Simplify

Courage, information, psychological preparation, and realism will help you achieve a fifth necessity in learning about technology—simplification.

Dr. Branscomb complains that many technical things have become so complicated that nontechnologists can't deal with them, and technologists have not worked hard enough to simplify or at least make more understandable these developments.

Complexity usually grows most unmanageable when a situation is fragmented. The publisher who changed production methods didn't integrate with the editors adequately. The editors didn't know the degree to which they would have to modify their layout. The changes upset some readers, so subscription renewals dropped, alarming the circulation department. The reduced press run, in turn, negated some of the savings in production, complicating production problems. The situation snowballed into complexities upon complexities, until it became nearly unmanageable. The problems could have been simplified if the publisher had known he was managing technological change and had integrated all the factors within his purview.

Dr. Tribus puts the matter this way: "It pays to remember that the man who is giving you technical information doesn't really know everything either. He just knows something. Then you combine that with what the marketing man says. Combining and integrating these—that's the manager's job. And if a manager can't help others communicate in these areas where he doesn't know as much as he'd like, he's not going to make it, is he?"

LEARNING TO MANAGE TECHNOLOGY

Dr. Tribus' question leads us to the crux—learning to manage technology. Let's look at five steps that will help you in this task:

1. Decide to manage

Many, if not most, generalist managers at first say they aren't qualified to manage technological change. They are especially uneasy at the prospect of running the technological lookout agency for the company. Isn't the research and development department better qualified? Probably, but with brilliant and heartening exceptions, it's not doing it, or not doing it well. On this subject, hear James R. Bright, professor of technology management and associate dean of the University of Texas' Graduate School of Business: [1]

"Discussions with several hundred research and engineering managers during the last eight years have convinced me that this role is played neither widely nor well in many R&D departments."

He sees three reasons for this:

■ Most R&D departments concentrate on product development and refinement and new applications. They don't look much beyond this narrow horizon. Management expectations, corporate custom, and tradition don't encourage them to study the technological environment beyond their immediate area.

■ Although some R&D and marketing managers recognize the need to survey technology on a broad basis, they lack support from higher levels to do it. When somebody does identify something significant beyond the ordinary range of interests, who will listen? He has trouble getting top management's ear except in the rare instance when he has a new product actually in hand.

■ The typical R&D, marketing, or engineering director seldom has a systematic methodology for assessing the innovative process. He may have access to technological capabilities, but not to the application of technology and its diffusion. Besides research, marketing, and engineering capabilities, technology is affected importantly by economics, sociology, politics, and ecology.

You may not perform the actual technological forecasting, but you can manage it, if you just make up your mind that you can

---

[1] Dr. Bright's direct and indirect quotations in this and the following chapter are taken from correspondence with the author and from his article, "Evaluating signals of technological change," *Harvard Business Review*, January–February 1970, Copyright 1970 by the President and Fellows of Harvard University.

do so. Learning about technology as outlined above should make you feel more at ease.

2. Integrate

Technology may generate a particular change, but many other factors usually become involved, and here the generalist manager finds it more comfortable.

"Xerography was not just a technological innovation," says Jacob Goldman, vice president and research director for Xerox. "It was also an innovation of marketing through leasing." It needed someone to correlate all the capabilities necessary to make the product a success.

Other kinds of integration will also make it easier for the generalist manager of technological change. Some companies have evolved formal programs. Honeywell Information Systems Inc., for instance, has one effective scheme. Line or production managers go into temporary leadership roles that actively involve them in the management of technical task forces. "We select managers who have reputations for accomplishment," explains Jerry Kanter, director of product marketing. "This arrangement usually works and we get a lot more agreement and dedication at the implementation stage."

Dr. William Duke, a technologist turned company president of Whittaker Corporation, says: "We favor a team approach—a group of functional specialists plus a natural leader. This allows us to superimpose product and market planning at the earliest phases of product research, and it makes technical team members more profit conscious."

Dymo Industries Inc. accomplishes such objectives with a once-a-month management report on R&D written in "absolute laymen's terms," says William Mullen, vice-president for research and development. Management meets informally with the R&D people regularly to discuss all projects under study. Twice a year, people from Dymo's locations that are overseas come in for the same purpose.

3. Humanize technology

"One can compensate for bad technology, to some extent, with great leadership, and for poor leadership with superb technology. But peak performance can never be achieved without peaks in both domains—the human and the technical." So says Henry M. Boettinger, director of management services for American Telephone & Telegraph Company.

The generalist manager can humanize technology—make it more relevant for ordinary people. Examples:

■ A doctor originated Coca-Cola as a patent medicine, in which guise it had limited sales and effectiveness. But nontechnical people noted its pleasant taste and used marketing techniques to develop it into a world-famous soft drink.

■ Over the engineering vice president's objections, the generalist president of a West Coast electronics firm reversed declining sales by assigning some of the engineers to accompany salesmen on calls involving complex problems. The idea worked, although its relevance escaped the technologist.

■ Benjamin Franklin was a generalist if ever one existed, and also one of the early technologists. He was a printer, journalist, pamphleteer, mailman, politician, diplomat, pioneer of electricity, founder of the physics of liquid surfaces, discoverer of the properties of marsh gas, inventor of bifocal spectacles and of improved fireplaces and stoves, advocate of watertight bulkheads on ships and of chimney shafts for the ventilation of mines. He humanized his technology, to the extent that his humanity is better remembered today than his technology.

Boettinger summarizes: "In the relevant future, organizations will experience a flood of sensory data and information. Their ability to think through—and about—this information to discern patterns of opportunity and potential harm will be taxed. . . . Future management of human-oriented, market-oriented technologies will be a rigorous contest. Yet I believe that it is one which can bring out the best in each of us."

4. Select strategies

Once you have decided to manage and applied a generalist's techniques of integration and humanization, you are ready for a managerial function common to all forms of management—selection of strategies.

Because this is a common managerial tool, we won't dwell on it, except to point out the technological implications. Even though separate technical events are unpredictable, you can spot forces shaping probable future developments which will affect the affairs of organizations and persons. Even if you deplore such developments, you must select strategies which, at the minimum, will prevent serious harm to your operation. At the maximum, you want to select strategies that will harness the forces for positive causes and purposes.

5. Make judgments

All managerial activities require this, too. Unless you will allow your operation to stagger from crisis to crisis, you must make judgments, based on a dispassionate appraisal of the possibilities ahead, far in advance of the actual events. Don't worry that such judgments may err in detail. Be content in the assurance that an organization which knows in general what to expect, even if details are wrong, will better survive than one which makes no preparations for fear of incorrect minutiae.

The entire matter of judgment about technology is so important that the entire next chapter will deal with it.

chapter seven

Influencing the Effects
of Technological Change

To master change, and not be mastered by it, we must "hasten the controlled, selective arrival of tomorrow's technologies," says Alvin Toffler in *Future Shock*.

Xerox's Dr. Myron Tribus states, "The key to the development of technology is managerial." Fundamental to such management is technological forecasting. Through the systematic use of an orderly technique, we can anticipate the major technological events that will affect our society significantly.

Only recently have managers realized the need to forecast technological change and its impact on their activities. We have long had economic forecasts, market forecasts, financial forecasts. Why not technological? The University of Texas' Dr. James R. Bright estimates that only one in five organizations participating in seminars he has conducted over four years, attended by more than 1,000 persons from industrial, academic, and governmental organizations, has started a forecasting effort, or even a continuous program.[1]

As you consider the potentials of technological predictions, ask yourself questions such as these:

- What should be my goals in such forecasting?
- How do I perform this task?
- How should I organize for it?
- What are the pitfalls of forecasting?
- How can forecasts be better used?

WHAT ARE MY GOALS?

The year 2000 is closer to us than the Depression, but many thinkers—economists, labor officials, and others—persist in thinking in terms of the 1930s. The past holds most of us like an anchor. Habit makes most of us look backward, not forward. One goal of forecasting is to change those habits.

Another goal is to explode myths about technology. Aurelio Peccei, Italian economist and industrialist, predicts that United States and European research and development will reach $73 billion annually by 1980, but note that he includes European spending in that total.

Most Americans believe that their society is the unchallenged leader of the world when it comes to the development and utilization of things technical. This may once have been true, but no longer. Several things indicate that Americans are not as inventive, compared to the rest of the developed world, as the myths would have us believe.

Dr. Tribus has tabulated patents per capita for a few nations

---

[1] Dr. Bright's direct and indirect quotations in this and the preceding chapter are taken from correspondence with the author and from his article, "Evaluating signals of technological change," *Harvard Business Review*, January–February 1970.

of the world, normalized so that the figure for the United States is 100. Although the data are for 1963, the latest year available, the situation since has probably grown poorer, according to the United States Commissioner of Patents:

United States. 100
United Kingdom 96
West Germany 175
Netherlands 181
Sweden 168
France 65
Belgium 65
Italy 31
Japan. 12

The employment of technical personnel in R&D is another indicator of how well a society will do in technology in the future. Dr. Tribus constructed the following table by taking 10 per cent of space and military R&D in the United States as applicable to the "civilian" economy, to show professional manpower during 1963 in civilian R&D (per unit of population, normalized to make the United States equal 100):

United States 100
United Kingdom 145
West Germany 95
Netherlands 157
Sweden 138
France 85
Belgium 82
Italy 33
Japan 125

All nations have shown an increase in technical effort since 1963 except the United States, which recently has shown a decline.

The decline has occurred because of economic troubles, and the disinclination of many American corporations to continue an expenditure such as R&D for which the payoff is ambiguous or far in the future.

Another goal of technological forecasting should be to minimize the ups and downs of R&D spending. IBM, with one of the best track records in research, spends between 5 and 8 per cent of sales on R&D. But most managers agree that there are no rules about the best way to budget for it. Texas Instruments' President Mark Shepherd, Jr., admits that "some of it is just subjective as hell." Raymond H. Herzog, president of Minnesota Mining & Manufacturing, points out that the natural lag in the results of research (typically four years even in a short-range project) means that the money that might pull a company out of a slump has already been spent. Pumping new funds into research in a crash effort, he says, is neither necessary nor—in most cases—very wise.

Despite such demurrals, most managers of technical activities call for more stability in R&D spending. A forecasting program can help.

Finally, the major purpose of technological forecasting is not necessarily to predict the actual form technology will take. As in other forecasts, the goal is to help evaluate the probability and significance of various possible future developments so that managers can make better decisions.

Technology is knowledge of physical relationships systematically applied to the useful arts. It can range from first intimations of how a basic phenomenon can be applied to solve a practical problem to an end product, device, or machine in an advanced operating system. Virtually any technology has a wide and relatively continuous range of characteristics in various applications over a period of time. This continuity makes technological forecasting possible.

While the forecaster cannot predict the exact nature and form the technology will take, except in a few immediate cases, he can cite probabilities about what performance characteristics a particular class of technology will provide by certain dates in the future. Furthermore, a good forecaster can analyze the implications of having these technical capacities ready in the future.

Consider technological forecasts as similar to market or economic forecasts. An experienced manager doesn't expect a marker prediction to hit the mark to the actual dollar. Yet he wants his market forecaster to be approximately right.

Take the case of the electric auto. Electric vehicles are, of course, technically feasible. For a time in the early 1920s, the electric auto challenged the internal-combustion vehicle. The battery-operated unit still powers some city delivery conveyances, industrial trucks, golf carts, and other specialized vehicles. But the technological forecast for electric autos remains negative despite the advantage of virtually pollution-free operation. The problems are cost, weight, and power—too high in the first two instances and too low in the latter.

So, technological forecasts thus far say "no" to the electric auto, but this may not remain the answer forever. Another goal for this activity is to keep monitoring the situation. Continuing change necessitates eternal vigilance.

HOW SHOULD I FORECAST?

There are many technological forecasting methods. For a summary of several, see *Technological Forecasting for Industry and Government* (Prentice-Hall, 1968), edited by Dr. Bright. He calls one (in the *Harvard Business Review*) "monitoring the environment for impending change." Studies of several dozen post-World War II innovations show that certain factors are nearly always present. He cites these:

■ A radical new technological advance is made visible to society first in written words, then in increasingly refined, enlarged, and more effective material forms, long before it achieves widespread usage.

■ The potential impact of the innovation is usually evident years before the new technology is in use on a scale great enough to affect existing conditions appreciably.

■ Social, political, and now to an increasing degree, ecological changes may alter the speed and direction of the innovation's progress.

■ Innovation may be abruptly influenced by decisions of key individuals who control supporting resources or determine policies that affect their application.

■ Technological capabilities—speed, power, miniaturization, strength, and capacity—increase exponentially over time once bottlenecks break. But they will begin to level off if they encounter scientific, economic, or social barriers. Failure to gage accurately this characteristic of acceleration is a principal reason why expert opinion from competent technologists, economists, and study groups so often proves to be wrong, according to Dr. Bright.

Dr. Bright believes that, with the exception of projects such as the development of the atom bomb, which was kept secret from 1942 to 1945 for security reasons, "it should be possible to monitor the environment to detect the coming, the progress, and the consequences of significant technological advances." By his definition, monitoring includes four activities:

1. Searching the environment for signals that may be forerunners of significant technological change.

2. Identifying the possible consequences (assuming that the signals aren't false and that the trends they suggest persist).

3. Choosing the parameters, policies, events, and decisions that should be observed and followed to verify the true speed and direction of technology and the effects of employing it.

4. Presenting the data from the foregoing steps in a timely and appropriate manner for management's use in decisions about the organization's reaction.

Here's a way to perform the technological forecasting task:

1. Inventory the important technological changes that you can see ahead; canvass others in the field for their opinions.

2. Arrange the list by relative importance; rearrange it accord-

ing to probability of occurrence; then rearrange it according to time of occurrence if the events do take place.

3. For those listed events which have a strong combination of importance and probability, attempt to state the potential impact on society.

4. For every event, separate the possible consequences into those that hold potential positive and negative impacts.

5. Analyze the events and then plan how to maximize the positive and minimize the negative impacts.

6. Organize to put the plan into effect.

If you can make anticipation an intellectual discipline, some basics should begin to surface soon. For example:

Extrapolation may turn up as the first principle. Again and again, businesses or professions greatly affected by technology are caught by surprise by some development. The reason usually lies in a failure to extrapolate.

Consider, again, the auto. The public and government show a growing concern about safety, air pollution, and traffic congestion. These concerns, together with technological developments, make it possible to extrapolate that future autos will be designed increasingly with problems of pollution, safety, traffic, and governmental pressures in mind in order to solve all four.

A second principle is the "imminent breakthrough." Take quantum electronics and the laser and maser. Now that technologists have learned to influence the energy states of atoms and molecules by radiation in new ways, and to withdraw stimulated and amplified emitted rays, we may expect to bring microminiaturization in electronics to new plateaus, including great decreases in size and weight and increases in the sophistication of the electrical effects that we can use. We may find new ways to use these processes to store, retrieve, and communicate information, and to extend man's vision and intellect and his ability to penetrate and affect matter.

The third principle of anticipation involves the "missing link."

Often in considering technological possibilities, we encounter a step we can't yet take. We see a final possibility on the horizon, but we don't know how to get there.

Here, we can at least write a description of what we need. We can tell a computer memory about the missing link, repeatedly telling it as science and technology advance.

An example is the computer. Thirty years ago, scientists understood the basic principle of the computer. Early computers using mechanical or vacuum tubes were available. However, something to replace tubes was the missing link. The computer needed so many tubes that the heat from the filaments within the tubes made their use prohibitive in anything but an experimental apparatus. Furthermore, the tubes proved unreliable, expensive, and too large.

The transistors and other semiconductors eventually came forth, to provide the missing link with a cheaper, smaller, cooler, and more reliable replacement for the vacuum tube. The computer business today rests largely on the fact that the missing link was found.

With the electric car, the missing link remains an electrical source from something lighter than present batteries. Often the missing link in a technical development is nontechnological. For example, atomic power can dig canals and harbors, but the public won't yet accept the nuclear explosion.

Sometimes the problem is an inadequate definition of the missing link. The supersonic transport (SST) was killed by Congress in the early 1970s, for instance, because of an almost total lack of such definition. Proponents failed to show the need for the plane and inadequately demonstrated how the SST would serve in the evolutionary development of future aircraft.

Technological forecasting may use a variety of techniques within the procedural framework suggested above. You must select the one or more that suit you best. One promising technique is *demand assessment*—the identification of important future needs which would be inadequately met by current technologies.

Examples include traffic control systems for autos and aircraft in major population centers, a synthetic source for protein in our diets, a method to recover oil easily and inexpensively from shale, a way or ways to lower steadily rising hospital costs.

Another method, the *theoretical limits test,* pushes a known apparatus or phenomenon to its theoretical limits and tries to visualize potential implications—both good and bad.

Consider the laser. The fact that light in a laser beam has a constant phase relationship has led to experiments to discover the implications of the phenomenon. One of the first technologies based on this marvel that has appeared is hologram photography—creation of three-dimensional images. Such a development holds obvious importance to photographic concerns. By extrapolating the characteristics of holograms, you can also see applications in cryptography, devices to store and display multidimensional information, engineering design, communication techniques, etc.

Parameter analysis, yet a different technique, goes to the heart of the forecasting process in predicting whether technical systems can reach or exceed key levels or parameters of performance by some future date. A celebrated example of a company that erred in parameter analysis is a successful maker of piston engines for aircraft. It ignored the jet field because it incorrectly reasoned that engine efficiency and fuel economy militated against jets ever replacing piston engines in commercial craft. Where it erred lay in the fact that jets can power bigger planes faster than piston engines, dramatically reducing the cost per ton mile and cost per seat mile.

Systems analysis can also help you to analyze technological futures, whereby the total environment is scrutinized. For example, an aerospace company entered the railroad-equipment business because its analysis showed that aerospace technology could be applied to the problems of rail passenger comfort, railroad speed, and economy.

Some forecasting techniques predict how competitors' technical actions will affect the company. When American Can Company acquired glass, paper, and plastics companies, competitors read that action as a shift from a "can company" to a "container company" concept, with profound technological implications.

Richard Rifenburgh, president of Mohawk Data Sciences Corporation, a maker of peripheral computer equipment, acknowledges that he follows the lead of competitors in research. "I want to trail a little to see on which frontier the volume is going to fall," he says. Nevertheless, the firm's line of ten devices in 1967 had expanded to more than sixty in 1971. Smaller companies, particularly, use this method, but all firms must watch the competition. They do it in marketing, finance, and many other areas. Why not in technology?

HOW SHOULD I ORGANIZE FOR TECHNOLOGICAL FORECASTING?

In general, the techniques you choose will influence your organization for technical predictions. Texas Instruments has an elaborate program called OST systems (objectives, strategies, tactics). The system is a formalized application of intuitive methods successful when it was much smaller in the early years of the company's phenomenal growth. Size brought with it a need to disperse these methods widely throughout the company. OST principles don't differ significantly from those that govern other well-managed innovative firms. What is unusual is the degree to which TI's procedures are written, circulated, and later used in measurement.

Top management states objectives for the corporation and for eight distinct businesses in which it is engaged in detailed, measurable, quantitative terms. The goals demand courses of action that get spelled out as formal strategies. Each of the strategies is assigned to a manager who makes a ten-year forecast of opportunities, identifies areas of likely innovation, and sets up checkpoints to measure progress. Special forms must be filled out, describing in detail who in the company is expected to do what, by what date.

In some cases, a company may hire outside scientists, technologists, or consulting firms to do the job for it. The outside course is most feasible if you wish scientific surveys to determine a variety of scientific disciplines' activity, promise, and relevance to your company's interests.

Another approach is the "wild men" technique—the delegation of forecasting to one or a few highly imaginative and active individuals to stimulate really new thoughts about technological potentials.

The most common approach is the in-company staff. Staff planning or program evaluation groups, such as General Electric's TEMPO organization, have been established with full-time responsibility for evaluating various technological futures and advising corporate and division managers about perceived opportunities and threats.

Long-range planning groups in other companies coordinate the development of technological forecasts in individual divisions.

Opportunity-seeking groups have been established in several chemical companies. They usually report either to top management or to the chief technical officer. They get in touch with current and potential customers to investigate how the company can help them solve technical problems and how some of the company's existing know-how can serve new applications. The groups are supposed to coordinate with marketing, but they are purposely given independent status so that they can delve into long-range problems instead of the near-term ones that marketing generally involves itself with.

Technical-information centers or commercial-intelligence units, another type of in-company staff, collect and evaluate data about technical trends.

WHAT ARE THE PITFALLS
OF FORECASTING?

Technological predictions appear subject to four principal short-comings which should be kept in mind.

1. *Unexpected interactions.* The interaction of two or more technical gains may lead to the totally unexpected. Post–World War II decisions to emphasize manned bombers rather than missiles failed to anticipate the interactions of higher-powered atomic weapons, the increased reliability and reduced size of solid-state devices, the capabilities of computers, and the development of new heat-resistant materials.

2. *Unprecedented demands.* An example of this is the computer. In the early 1950s experts estimated that only about thirty electronic computers would be needed to handle all the calculations then being made by every bookkeeper, scientist, and technologist in the United States. This apparent lack of demand kept many potential manufacturers out of the field. Actually, the computer made possible calculations and uses never before imagined. The dry-copying device is another example. The Xerox and other units didn't merely take over the existing photocopying market. It created an entirely new market, changing typing practices, report distributions, use of published materials, etc.

3. *Major discoveries.* Important developments—the transistor effect, superconductivity, lasers, steroid activity, to name a few—have opened totally unexpected technological opportunities.

Both the shortcomings of imagination and the randomness of scientific discovery will undoubtedly keep forecasters' batting averages low in anticipating those major breakthroughs in entirely new phenomena.

4. *Inadequate data.* This is probably the factor that most limits technological forecasting. Fortunately, thanks to the computer, data supply is improving. However, forecasters often must develop some of their own figures before going on.

Herbert Hollomon of MIT, who spent fifteen years with General Electric before serving as Assistant Secretary of Commerce for Science and Technology under Presidents Kennedy and Johnson, believes that few companies are sufficiently receptive to the results of their own research. "They often set it aside," he says. "They never really decide what they would do if it were successful." While in Washington, Dr. Hollomon directed a study of the many small independent electronic firms that sprung up in the 1950s and 1960s along Route 128 outside Boston and concluded that many were started by frustrated scientists and engineers from bigger companies. Most of the small, specialized firms would not have existed but for the failure of larger corporations to exploit ideas and forecasts that were theirs for the using.

James Brian Quinn, business consultant and professor of business administration at Dartmouth College's Amos Tuck School of Business Administration, offers four suggestions for integrating decisions better with forecasts:

1. Forecasts should develop the pragmatic insights needed to make this year's decisions—not focus on esoteric problems of the year 2000. This doesn't mean that you should not look to or beyond 2000, but do it in the context of the decision you have to make this year.

2. Forecasters should place opportunities and threats in an appropriate order of priority. This will encourage action. It's easier to do something about one thing at a time. The human tendency is to do nothing when you're faced with unorganized opportunities and threats.

3. Forecasts should be fitted in with the company's regular cycles of executive decision. About 90 per cent of most companies' expenditures are committed during periodic budget reviews, so this is the crucial time to submit technological forecasts.

4. Promising executives, wherever possible, should be exposed

to planning and forecasting activities. Most management men today have had little meaningful background in technological affairs. With the world increasingly dominated by technology, they should remedy that gap in their background. Exposure to forecasting is one way.

In addition, nontechnical men may make excellent forecasters. It's an historical fact that highly qualified technical people rarely make good predictors of the future. Technical people who understand the problems are likely to assume that much time will be needed for the solution, while nontechnical people often exhibi. childlike faith that the experts can solve almost any problem. Then, the technical people sometimes go on to prove the nontechnical people correct.

Technological forecasting is relatively new. Like any new activity, it has its proponents and detractors. The question is not: Should I do technological forecasting? It is: How should I do it? One chapter can't do the subject full justice. For one of the best overviews on formal technological forecasting, see Robert U. Ayres' *Technological Forecasting and Long-range Planning* (McGraw-Hill Book Company, 1969). You may not agree with his speculation, "It may be that science itself is to be the new religion of the world." But you do have to agree with him that technology is a powerful instrument of change.

If you wish to influence that change, you must start with forecasting.

part three

Methods Change

chapter eight

Change in Methods

Henry Ford the elder invented nothing, but he was a true innovator—primarily of methods changes which led to mass production.

Methods change is a familiar phrase in labor relations circles where its narrow definition relates to changes usually resulting from technological shifts. But here it's used in the broader connotation—changes in the ways of doing things that are not primarily technological, even though they may have been generated in the beginning by technical forces.

Case in point: The computer, a technological change, has led to many methods changes in office procedures. The new office techniques in themselves often contain little that's technical, even though they stem basically from the computer.

Economist Peter Drucker, a professor at New York University, estimates that for every $1 spent to achieve innovation, $10 has to be spent to develop it into a product, process, or service. Much of that added $10 goes for methods changes—in marketing, servicing, distributing, and a host of other functions essentially not technical.

We have seen how the concept of leasing contributed almost as much to the success of Xerox as the actual technical invention of the dry photocopying process. This change in marketing methods has a parallel in the carpeting industry.

Textile firms specializing in carpeting were in trouble. Their suppliers of synthetic fibers were worried. In cooperation with banks and other financial institutions, the chemical companies came up with a new marketing method. Instead of selling carpeting after the new-home buyer had purchased his dwelling, they went to the builders, persuading them to install the carpeting in the house or apartment condominium before it was sold and include its cost in the original price of the residence and in the mortgage payments. The idea proved such a boon to carpeting manufacturers that makers of other home products, notably major appliances, have adopted it and experienced comparable successes with it.

On a broader scale, basic technological changes may lead to methods changes in the social area with vital results. Although we tend toward extreme pessimism about conditions in America, technology gives us grounds for optimism. When the story of the application of science and technology to the problems of society is penned a century or so from now, the 1970s may be noted as the period in which a pronounced and significant shift began to take place in balancing technological and social advance.

The importance of methods changes to follow up on what is usually technological change is illustrated by the case of Great Britain. In the past quarter century, Britain has developed antibiotics, radar, and the jet engine. The computer also owes much to British technical skill. Yet Great Britain has not reaped the expected rewards from any of these products. One reason is a failure in marketing methods.

Of twenty-nine products developed largely in one nation, the United States can claim credit for nineteen and Western European countries for ten. But the United States led in the sale of twenty-two and Western European nations in only seven. Western European marketing methods did not match American. An example, again, is leasing. European makers of computers were slow to adopt this method of marketing. American firms, especially IBM, used the financing device widely and marketed the expensive machines more successfully than did the European competitors who tried at first to sell them in the conventional way.

NEW METHODS TO FOLLOW
NEW TECHNOLOGY

Evidence mounts that the 1970s are experiencing a period of anti-technology. Congressional refusal to provide government funding for the SST is one among many such indications. As we have already pointed out in the previous section, we need more, not less, technology, provided it is well directed. Furthermore, history proves that it's difficult, if not impossible, to stop technology.

Yet the fact remains that ecological and other environmental arguments against technology may temporarily curb it or at least change its course. A manager of change in the decade of the 1970s will be wise to turn more of his attention to other aspects of change. New methods will prove one fruitful field. Furthermore, the strong current trend toward a service economy in the United States encourages emphasis on methods changes because service industries rely more on improved methods than do manufacturing industries, who traditionally have focused mostly, although not exclusively, on technology.

By 1975, 70 per cent of the jobs in the United States will be in service or government. The proportions have almost exactly transposed since 1930, when 70 per cent of employment was in manufacturing. About two-thirds of the new jobs being created between 1970 and 75 will be in government and services. Efficiency will take on new meaning in the era of service and whatever follows that. Some believe that a period of psychic fulfillment will evolve from the present service economy. Examples already exist:

■ Psychic services like TWA's "foreign accent" flight where decor and food of the flight are in French or whatever is the country of destination. At least one American barber shop now offers movies while you get your hair cut.

■ Simulated environments to recreate Japanese Geisha houses of the eighteenth century or the atmosphere of Elizabethan England.

■ Live environments like the African safari.

■ New kinds of businesses that provide psychological services —consultants who specialize in employee motivation, sales, design, etc.

The foregoing examples primarily involve changes in methods, not technology. And such instances basically pertain to man's mental approach to doing things. There are also physical methods changes. We'll discuss instances of each.

MENTAL METHODS CHANGES

Changes in attitude constitute one of the common types of men tal method shifts. Many manufacturing companies, as a case in point, must change their mental attitudes toward service activities. Despite the fact that General Electric has been an electrical manufacturer since 1887, it has turned increasingly to other areas that relate only indirectly to the original electrical business. It has a financing activity in its General Electric Credit Corporation. It has joined with Time Inc. to form an educational subsidiary, General Learning Corporation. It's in the entertainment business with a wholly owned Tomorrow Entertainment, Inc. It's a leader in computer time-sharing services. All these ventures result from a change in mental attitudes—new methods.

Here are other examples of changes in attitude:

■ In the late 1950s, Thomas D. Coe founded Wakefield Engineering Company in Wakefield, Massachusetts, even before he had a product to make and sell. Yet his unconventional approach worked because he started out as a contract manufacturer, offering to produce almost anything the customer wanted. Today, he has a thriving firm producing heat sinks—because, initially, he changed from the ordinary way of starting a new business.

■ Until recently, bakeries normally bought flour in 100-pound sacks. But the Illinois Central Railroad and Omar Bakeries adopted a new attitude toward this routine. The result: Flour is now delivered to Omar—and other large bakeries—in covered railroad hopper cars. This method eliminates packaging, weighing, and handling the sacks. The cars are sealed against dust and have smooth inside surfaces. A vacuum process sucks the flour from the cars.

To change your mental attitudes:

1. Counteract the symptoms of perceptual block. Be conscious of your own reactions to what seems to be a familiar problem, and be aware of the ways in which such a reaction manifests itself.

2. Take your time in reaching conclusions. An individual with a perceptual block tends to short-circuit and to jump to conclusions too rapidly.

3. Watch out for the routine. This does not mean avoiding ordinary assignments; rather, it means avoiding the ordinary mental attitude toward routine tasks.

We tend to label familiar objects or actions as "obvious" or "trivial." Thus we lose the faculty of being able to examine them clearly and objectively. Two men stalled their car while driving up a slight incline on a snowy day. Struggling to put chains on the vehicle, they noticed another car stopped a short distance ahead. They watched in amazement as the car's driver proceeded to the side of the road and began to roll large snowballs, which she then placed in the trunk of her car. She entered the car and drove away; the weight of the snowballs gave the car traction so that it could move forward. The other driver changed her attitudes in a solution which the two men might well have dismissed as ridiculous had it been suggested to them.

Another mental method change we should make is our attitude toward questions and answers, or decisions. With us in the West, all the emphasis is on the answer to the question. Most of our books on decision making develop systematic approaches to finding an answer.

Yet there's another way. The Japanese believe that the important element is defining the question. They consider that the crucial steps are to decide whether there's a need for a decision and what the decision is about. To the Japanese, this step becomes the essence of the decision. The answer to the question—what the West considers the decision—follows the definition.

During the process leading to the decision, the Japanese make no mention of what the answer might be. They do this to avoid forcing people to take sides. Once people take sides, a decision would be a victory for one side and a defeat for the other. So, the focus is on finding what the decision is really about, not what the decision should be. It results in a meeting of the minds that there is—or is not—a need to change behavior.

The Japanese approach to a question takes time, which exasperates most Westerners. But when the question is defined and a consensus reached, action usually takes place with amazing speed —far more rapidly than in the West because everybody agrees on the action and no time is lost trying to "sell" any of the recalcitrant but powerful people who must be parties to the decision.

To illustrate how this works, consider Toyo Rayon, the largest Japanese manufacturer of man-made fibers. It made nothing but rayon as late as the mid-1950s. Then it decided to switch to synthetic fibers. But it didn't phase out rayon making as all Western firms in a similar situation have done. It closed its rayon mills overnight. Its decision probably was the right one, for it has prospered since. It was able to take such drastic action because it started by defining the question rather than answering it immediately.

The Japanese method almost guarantees that all the alternatives get consideration. It postpones commitment until management has determined all the ramifications of the decision. This method may lead to wrong answers to problems, but rarely to right answers to the wrong problems. The latter, as decision makers know, is the most dangerous course, leading to the irretrievably erroneous decision.

This approach is especially useful for major matters. It is probably too cumbersome for most minor questions.

A third mental method change should help with those small situations, as well with the large: Focus more on goals than on time in change management.

Americans, particularly, tend to make time all-important in changing situations. Actually, time may not even have secondary importance, but the goal always should take first billing. The following case study shows what happens when priorities become transposed.

Management of a midwestern firm decided that their monthly employee magazine needed to be changed to meet shifting conditions in employment and product mix. To avoid skipping an issue, the manager of employee communication put a rush on the project. When the editors produced a new version of the house organ without skipping an issue, all the people involved congratulated themselves on managing a good change.

But after only seven issues, it became apparent that the new magazine did not meet objectives. Readers were not enthusiastic about it, and management complained that it did not motivate employees as much as they had hoped it would.

In developing still another version of the magazine, the editors suspended publication for three months. They interviewed all in top management, editors of other house organs, and outside magazine consultants. On the second time around, they defined and refined their goals, taking sufficient time to design a magazine that would meet the objectives.

Even though publication was suspended for three months, this proved unimportant. Employees welcomed the second new version of the house organ with more enthusiasm. It was successful. In reality, it took ten months to come up with a satisfactory new magazine—three months in which goals were defined and seven months in which the editors went down a dead end.

A fourth type of mental method change is an attitude toward change itself. There can be no change until there is an advocate of change. Somebody must want it. We'll have much more to say on this in Part Five. Now we can point out that all managers want to improve their operations, but some drag their feet on proposed shifts because their personal attitudes interfere with their business judgment.

Even if personal factors didn't interfere, many business forces complicate the typical breakthrough—the company climate, the past record of change, and the extent of preoccupation with keeping the status quo and avoiding bad changes.

Don't underestimate the power of such business forces. In a recent twelve-month period in the chemical industry, 540 new products were proposed; 92 were judged pertinent; 8 were approved for development; but only 1 finally went to market.

The advocate of change must overcome the negative forces. Often he is not the man who had the first idea for change. Many bright, creative people don't have the political skills to pilot a change past shoals. The wheel gets turned over to the new advocate with the political moxie.

Good advocates think "futures." They are long-range planners, who know that such planning is a process directed toward making today's decisions with tomorrow in mind and a means of preparing for future decisions so that they may be made rapidly, economically, and with as little disruption to the business as possible.

What is the future? How long is long range? The only answer for a manager of change is something that sounds facetious at first but which is actually decidedly serious. Five years is generally accepted as long range because six years is too long and four years is too short.

Of course, long range varies with circumstances. A pulp and paper company has to plan its timber needs forty years in advance. But the maker of a fad product like hula hoops may consider six months a long time.

A manager of long-range future change tends to think in technological terms, but methods metamorphoses stretch out far, too. Example: A methods change may be to establish a long-term mechanism to implement change. General Learning Corporation, like many companies, has a New Ventures Operation whose function is to launch new activities. It searches them out, evaluates them, then starts them and manages them until they are established, when a permanent organization takes over. The New Ventures Operation may have the responsibility for a year or longer, but its role is not to manage the new activity forever. Once established, it turns it over so that it can go on to something else because it's a mechanism or method for future change.

PHYSICAL METHOD CHANGES

The foregoing method changes relate primarily to mental, attitudinal or psychological shifts. Yet physical changes in method are vital, too. Here are examples in the marketing area:

■ Light-bulb manufacture in the U.S. has increased by more than 400 per cent over the past thirty-five years, but during the period population in the country has climbed 55 per cent. While some of the increase has resulted from technology, much of it has also resulted from new marketing methods that developed new uses for artificial light in decorative effects and in heating.

■ Foamite Firefoam is a product that originated with MacAndrews & Forbes Co., a dealer and processor of licorice root. The traditional processing method was to extract the licorice by adding soda ash. This resulted in a liquid of startling foaming power. This foam had been a nuisance until a change advocate with an eye toward marketing remembered that a fire dies when deprived of oxygen. The foam residue spread rapidly, cutting off oxygen. Why not try it as an agent to put out fire? It worked, and MacAndrews & Forbes developed a new use with a new marketing method.

■ Sometimes the revised marketing method involves recognition of new economic conditions. Sears, Roebuck & Co., for instance, developed its mail-order business after recognizing that the nation's farm population had dramatically improved its economic status and wanted a way to buy the same types of goods and services available to its urban brethren.

■ Americans want greater diversity in their clothing, shelter, and transportation. New methods, often combined with technology, can give it to them. Take the case of Ford's Mustang: 3 (bodies) × 4 (engines) × 3 (transmissions) × 4 (basic sets of engine modifications) = 144 different combinations, not counting one rock-bottom six-cylinder model to which modifications don't apply and two Shelby and racing setups. Add to this all the different color and accessory options and you get 25 million different combinations possible on just one new family sports car.

New marketing methods require three elements:

1. Systematic organization of effort to sell, deliver, and get paid for a product.

2. A look at the entire business from the viewpoint of its ultimate purpose and justification—thus, from the customers' viewpoint.

3. Recognition that marketing methods need as much change as manufacturing or any technologically oriented aspect of business.

As we have already noted, the computer has revolutionized office procedures. Yet changes in office methods may come in a more mundane way. Visualize this scene:

You have a report to submit to your boss by noon. It's important that it be free of typographical errors. Three different secretaries have already proofread the typescript. As you give it a final reading, you puzzle over what one of the secretaries intended in her marginal note. Unfortunately, all three made their correction notations in pencil, and you must waste valuable time determining the originator.

How do you make sure that you won't waste time in the future, because you have many such reports with tight deadlines? Have each secretary make her notations in a different, distinctively colored pencil. With this simple device, you have made a change (and an improvement) in office procedures.

You can evolve methods changes on the factory floor, too, that don't rely basically on technology. General Motors Corporation provides its employees the following "think list" to spur ideas for change in the use of machinery:

1. Can a machine be used to do a better or faster job?
2. Can the fixture now in use be improved?
3. Can materials handling for the machine be improved?
4. Can a special tool be used to combine the operations?
5. Can the quality of the part being produced be improved by changing the sequence of the operation?
6. Can the material used be cut or trimmed differently for greater economy or efficiency?
7. Can the operation be made safer?
8. Can paperwork regarding this job be eliminated?
9. Can established procedures be simplified?

As these questions suggest, change sometimes requires that you come up with a series of observed attributes which you meld and weld into a new method for doing a job.

Adaptations of attributes may occur in one or more of several different ways. For instance, they may occur as the result of:

■ A discovery—A perception for the first time of something whose existence was hitherto unknown. In the area of methods, the invention of writing was a discovery.

■ An innovation—A new or novel element applied to an existing way of doing something. The computer was an innovative kind of change.

■ A synthesis—A different mixture of known elements or parts to make a new whole. The Dewey Decimal system in library cataloging changed library science beyond recognition. It synthesized a logical system for cataloging with an existing collection of books. Now used throughout the United States in general libraries, it enables the library patron to find his way around almost any standard library in America.

■ A mutation—An alteration in the form or qualities of an existing entity or concept. Technological changes in printing now enable an unskilled clerk to turn out professional-quality printing in the office—a methods mutation that has revolutionized the functions and responsibilities of many clerical perople.

COMBINING MENTAL AND PHYSICAL METHODS CHANGES

Often a methods change contains elements of both mental and physical factors in it. You can see this combination most clearly in "systems" changes. In a systems approach all informational, behavioral, scientific, and engineering disciplines are used in concert to bear on a problem.

The systems approach is valuable as a technique of change because it views all elements of a situation as a unified whole—at least ideally.

An automobile system is more than the car. It includes roads, gas stations, accessories, parts, etc. But because it was developed piecemeal, it has many faults. Air transport is another example of a piecemeal approach.

An example of a challenge needing systems where new methods, as well as technology, will figure in the solution is BOSNYWASH, the urban-transport problem in the Boston-New York-Washington corridor. Basic to the systems approach are statistics and probabilities. How many people will want to move around BOSNYWASH? When? Where? How? How about weekends vs. weekdays? Summer vs. winter? What price are they willing to pay for public vs. private-car transport?

Cost and time measures must be put on everything in a systems change. If you can't measure specifically, measure by probabilities. When you have the numbers, you can figure tradeoffs.

No wonder that the computer is a major tool in systems change. It can work to a mathematical model to determine the optimum number of stops for a commuter railroad, for example.

Some things—nationwide airline reservations, for instance—couldn't be accomplished at all without a systems approach where a kind of synergism occurs. The blending of many disciplines leads to a sum greater than its parts. Methods changes—both mental and physical—combine with technology to produce a system that permits the air traveler to line up a trip from New York to Chicago to Denver to Los Angeles to Phoenix and back to New York in just a few minutes—provided he doesn't have to wait in line behind other travelers with similarly complicated itineraries, of course.

The systems approach, however, will fail: (1) when too large a problem is embraced, (2) where too precise a solution is sought, (3) if too many unknown factors—usually human elements—exist.

Essential to an effective systems approach (and to managing change of whatever kind) is a good flow of information. Information lies at the heart of managing change because only with good facts can you anticipate change, and thus effectively manage it.

chapter nine

Strategy for Methods Change

"O God, give us the serenity to accept those things we cannot change, the courage to change those things that can be changed, and the wisdom to know the difference."

This ancient prayer is especially applicable to people interested in changing methods of accomplishing work—which should include every manager worth his pay.

PREDICTING THE NEED FOR CHANGE

How do you predict the need for a methods change? No specific rules provide foolproof indications, but the following events give clues that a methods change should at least be investigated:

- When your costs are rising.
- When employee turnover increases significantly in a year.

- When errors increase or quality decreases.
- When your technology, product, or service changes significantly.
- When you haven't changed your methods substantially in at least three years.
- When the competition changes its methods.
- When two or more employees suggest the need for change in the same area.
- When productivity declines.
- When business volume drops.
- When profits dip.

As in technology, you can also organize a special task force or other group whose function it is to predict the need for methods change. Aetna Life and Casualty Company, Hartford, Conn., formed such a unit, the Productivity Systems Department, to monitor the need for change in office procedures.

Man generally gets his new insights by:

- Accidental discovery
- Experience
- Imports
- Systematic observation and analysis

In managing change of any kind, but especially in the area of methods, American business must rely increasingly on the last technique. *Accident* is too haphazard and infrequent. We are changing so rapidly now that *experience* no longer is as reliable as in the past. In methods of doing things, Americans are usually so far ahead of the rest of the world that *imports* help little. (As already indicated, this is not the case in technology. As we shall see, neither is it the case in changes involving organization and people.)

In *systematic observation,* you can predict the need for change by taking the following steps:

■ *Train people to do the job.* We train people to perform research in scientific and technological areas. Why not in the fields of methods, too? True, many companies employ methods engineers, but these people usually confine themselves to new methods for using machinery or equipment. Needed are experts who can perform in a broader range that goes beyond conventional time and motion study—in office procedures, employee relations, marketing, etc.

■ *Provide them with special facilities.* The broad-methods expert may merit a laboratory or comparable aid, just as the scientist does. With the aid of a small staff, a company psychologist performed motivation research in a southern textile plant and learned that hourly employees improved their output with increased responsibility. A group of twenty skilled employees were offered responsibility for all the planning, scheduling, and control functions. When they needed help, they were permitted to call on the foreman or any of the other people who had performed the planning and other technical functions. Leadership arose from within the group. The research project was accomplished under carefully controlled and observed circumstances, with the psychologist in charge and offering consulting help. One direct result of the concept was a 33 per cent savings in overhead.

■ *Give methods people access to special information.* This proves advisable for the same reason that you provide them with special facilities. An illustration of how this can pay off: Researchers for the Encyclopedia Britannica's marketing department asked themselves what non-English-speaking nations in the world had high proportions of people who could read English. The answer: Several Western European nations and Japan. Various considerations, including xenophobia, ruled out a strong sales effort for the English-language Britannica in Western Europe, but not in Japan. In one recent year, Britannica sold more English-language sets in Japan than in Great Britain. Another payoff from this special information led to the decision to prepare foreign-language editions in some European languages.

■ *Detach the function from day-to-day operations,* just as you detach the lab from other activities in technology. The southern textile mill didn't begin to receive substantial benefits from its psychologist until it detached him from the employee-relations activity and gave him a small staff of his own.

GETTING METHODS CHANGED

In typical large or medium-sized companies, the method needing change usually involves more than one department. The knowledge required often is complex, and special effort must be taken to get it disseminated and applied. Thus you need a team effort to guide the change, disseminate it, and apply it. Sometimes you will need specialists to do the detailed work associated with the team effort.

Let's see how this will work out—in the case of clerical productivity. "Increases in salary do not, per se, cause increases in employee performance," says Joseph A. Fazio, Aetna Life and Casualty's training consultant for productivity systems. "In fact, some motivation experts go so far as to include salary as a job dissatisfier. They liken it to hunger in that its impact is temporary. Man is hungry, eats, and is satisfied, but becomes hungry again."

However, the proper form of monetary compensation can be an excellent motivator. Fazio believes the proper form for many and possibly most office employees is incentive pay, and his company has forty-five years' experience with incentives to support his contention.

Since 1926, Aetna has had clerical productivity measurement programs, together with incentive bonuses. These programs have grown the most during the last ten years, mushrooming from about 700 employees under measurement in 1960 to more than 4,000 in 1970.

"Basically, the plan is designed to save the company money," Mr. Fazio says. "The resulting savings are shared with those employees who contributed to these savings." In 1969, clerical people under measurement shared more than $2 million in incentive payments. Net savings to the company were $7.2 million.

One success story involved Participating Annuity Life Insurance Company (PALIC), McLean, Va., acquired by Aetna in 1967. PALIC faced a continual backlog in policy issue, lack of adequate space for staff additions, and an anticipated marked increase in its workload.

When it showed interest in work measurement and incentive pay, Aetna's Productivity Systems Department ran a feasibility study on PALIC's policy-issue functions and found that this operation fulfilled the three prerequisites for individual work measurement:

- Rate of production controlled by the person doing the work
- Relatively continuous supply of work
- Definite procedures for processing work

As the study continued, specialists uncovered work flow inefficiencies. They established work standards, along with an incentive pay scale under which the incentives were paid weekly.

Before the new system, employees had processed an average of 11 new contracts per day. In the first week under incentives, the average jumped to 23.6.

"Backlogged work was reduced to the point where the section was considered as operating on a current basis," Mr. Fazio reports. "In fact, for a substantial amount of time some personnel had no work to do, indicating the potential existed for absorbing an increase in workload with the present staff."

The program had its first complete audit twelve weeks after it was started. By then, the staff had been reduced 32 per cent through normal turnover and transfers. This reduction of nine employees added up to an annual $45,000 cut in salaries, excluding benefits. The first thirteen weeks also saw the processing time for a policy cut from nine days to two.

Clerical productivity offers a rich lode for methods changes because it climbed only 4 per cent during the 1960s, in contrast to an 83 per cent rise during that same decade for production employees.

In this and other successful methods-improvement programs, you as the innovator can usually do the job most effectively in this sequence:

1. *Pick the task to improve.* In PALIC's case, this wasn't difficult, but sometimes it proves the most troublesome part of the entire effort. A distributor of industrial supplies decided that a revised sales incentive plan would spur lagging sales. Instead, the new program so demoralized the sales staff that volume fell still more drastically. Eventually, it turned out that the problem was an obsolete product line, not sales incentives. To maximize your changes of picking the right task for your attention:

■ Devise ways to test your decision in advance. Canvass your employees—they may know more about the problem than you do.

■ Read the literature in the field on the problem. Where has it cropped up before? What did others do about it? Did attention to it lead to improvements?

■ Seek advice from outsiders in areas where you lack expertise. Mistakes often occur in the region of the innovator's blind spot. If you have had little experience in marketing—a common Achilles heel of innovators—obtain counsel in that area.

■ Review alternate tasks to improve. Apply the foregoing tests to them.

2. *Study the task to improve.* Aetna's Productivity Systems Department did so with efficiency, but many innovators slip up here. They do it hurriedly or superficially. For instance, a new incentive sales plan may well be the right objective, but it could

be so poorly studied that the wrong new plan results. An example of careful study involved Hydroculture, Inc., a Phoenix, Arizona, firm specializing in the commercial development of hydroponics, the cultivation of plants in water containing dissolved inorganic nutrients rather than in soil. It had a problem with pollination. The pollination function normally is performed by wind or bees or even birds which shake and vibrate pollen free from the base of the flower so that it settles on the pistil. But hydroponics is accomplished in greenhouses with no wind, bees, or birds. Hydroculture studied the problem and determined that the vibrating feature of a cordless electric toothbrush would accomplish the pollination. It tried several brands and finally selected General Electric's because the charge lasted longest. In forty-five minutes, it could pollinate some 1,100 plants on one charge.

3. *Challenge everything.* A young bus driver challenged the accepted belief that expensive buses of a transportation company had to remain idle on Sundays. He devised "Mystery Tours" for weekend excursions in which the buses would journey to nearby points of interest. We tend to accept the established way of doing things. Get into the mental habit of constant skepticism.

4. *Work out a better way.* Aetna worked one out for PALIC. Hydroculture did likewise in coming up with the toothbrush for pollination. A fundamental truth is this: If you know what your problem is, if you have studied it, and if you have challenged all established ways of doing things you usually *can* work out a better way.

5. *Apply the new way.* To fail to apply the new way is analogous to the salesman who doesn't ask for the order. Yet, it happens in both instances.

6. *Follow up.* The audit often constitutes a handy way to follow up. Aetna used the audit, partly to find out how the methods changes were working out, but also to follow up and make sure that no backsliding had occurred. It's common to slip back

to old ways of doing things even when new methods have been proved definitely superior.

The necessity for follow-up is particularly acute in methods changes. With technology, you deal largely with tangibles, but the intangible figures more prominently in the area of methods. You can't see, hear, touch, or smell the intangible. Its ephemeral quality troubles many and makes changes more difficult in this area. One way to handle the intangible successfully is to deal more effectively with psychological aspects of methods changes. Here are some guidelines.

1. *Take the initiative.* Robert Benchley, the satirist and essayist, put it this way: "I could build a bridge if only someone would get me started."

Initiative is a state of mind, the welcoming of a possible new adventure, a new experience. To get started:

■ Put ideas in writing. Carry a small notebook and pencil with you at all times, even by your bed at night. Jot down those stray thoughts as they occur. Develop a filing system and file the ideas for later reference. An added advantage of putting ideas in writing and filing them away is that you discipline your thoughts by doing this, avoiding the vague ones that don't pass muster when you try to put them into words.

■ Get a lot of ideas. Novelist Somerset Maugham contended that "people who conceive few [ideas] find it very difficult not to regard them with inordinate respect." Many people seize hold of one idea, then spend much time and effort trying to prove, disprove, or develop it. If they disprove the idea, they have to tool up all over again. But even if they prove it, they still haven't really learned whether a better idea exists because they have closed up shop.

■ Be aggressive. Your conscious mind must play an active, attacking role in pursuing ideas for methods changes. Initiative requires constant effort, even aggressive strain.

2. *Be persistent.* In the course of any move toward change, a lessening of persistence frequently occurs—because of repeated failures, lack of energy, or other reasons. You must learn to cope with this reaction. Many of the suggestions for initiative apply here, too, plus these others:

■ Take pains. Innovation is the capacity for taking infinite pains. "All the genius I have lies in this," wrote Alexander Hamilton. "When I have a subject in hand, I study it profoundly. Day and night it is before me. What people are pleased to call the fruit of genius is the fruit of labor and thought." If you take pains, you guard against the possibility of failure, the factor which most commonly lessens persistence.

■ Get away from it all when interest flags. Take a break. Do something different. You may find that working on several projects for methods change at once can stimulate, not confuse you.

■ Get the facts. We have already dealt with this, but now we can examine another aspect: When do you have enough facts, when will persistence no longer pay off sufficiently? Some clues to the answer: When the facts start repeating, when new facts come much more slowly, when you run out of time. The extra time spent in trying to come up with the "final fact" usually is not worth it. The "final fact" may not improve the idea at all— or it may add to it so microscopically that only experts could detect it.

3. *Give your curiosity full range.* The innovative person must retain intense curiosity about everything and an expectant responsive attitude toward life in general. This develops an unconscious mind stocked with a wide variety of information. Much of what we know, learn, or observe in a specific context proves applicable to many problems and extendable by endless variations and combinations. Curiosity needs exercise. If you try to unlimber it just for the problem at hand, odds are that it won't yield much if you haven't been using it regularly. It needs action just as your body does. Read books by unfamiliar authors. Study unfamiliar fields. Meet new people. Ask why.

4. *Simplify.* When you work with many intangible factors typical of a methods change, you must deal with a variety of half-ideas, wisps of suggestions, half-formless situations. You must put all these into usable order. How? Here are a few suggestions:

■ Orient the impressions. Find a common denominator for them. Write down first impressions of what the problem is. Next, list every factor you can think of that could be part of that problem. Rearrange these factors into logical relationships and sequences. Look for the key factor. Also try writing the problem in as many ways as you can imagine. Or try to explain it to a person unfamiliar with it. Or concentrate on elements of the problem you can control yourself.

■ Ask perceptive questions. If the problem is to improve a service, questions like these may serve: Can we improve the service's function, make it do more things? Can we get higher performance—do it quicker, more cheaply? Can we increase its salability?

■ Evaluate the impressions. The abc's of evaluating ideas are these: (*a*) Give them a loose evaluation, screening them roughly for categories—such as "limited possibility," "just possible," "impossible," and so on. (*b*) Tighten up on the immediately possible groups. Set up criteria for judging more closely—for instance, simplicity, compatibility with human nature, timeliness, explainability, interest, suitability, feasibility, acceptability. Tailor your criteria to your problem. With the problem of service improvement, for example, the good criteria might be timeliness, suitability, feasibility, acceptability, and compatibility with human nature. (*c*) Next consider possibilities to improve or develop the basic idea. Ask questions such as: Is this the simplest way to do it? Is each part of this idea necessary? Will all publics accept it? What has been overlooked?

■ Control the volume. The conscious mind can cope with the mass of impressions its unconscious mind delivers to it by eliminating the extraneous thoughts. Your evaluation procedures will help here. Discipline, too, will assist. Don't let yourself woolgather. Avoid blind alleys.

YOUR CHANGE QUOTIENT

Ask yourself the following questions to determine your mind's change quotient. The queries apply for any kind of change, but they relate particularly to methods change with its psychological emphasis:

1. Can you get enthusiastic about problems outside your specialized area?

2. Do you feel the excitement and challenge of finding a solution to problems in many areas, regardless of whether they are major or minor challenges?

3. When a problem seems to hold little or no interest, do you nevertheless try to develop an interest and stimulation in the problem's possibilities?

4. Do you know what is expected of you by management?

5. Do you seldom assume limitations and lack of freedom in your work?

6. Do you recognize flagging persistence for what it is and set the problem aside temporarily, without closing your mind to it or giving up?

7. Do you resist "blocking" a project, even though you think it trivial and distracting from problems more to your taste?

8. Do you accept the occasional illogic of your mind, recognizing that it can help lead you to solutions in managing change?

9. Do you commonly carry a notebook to put stray ideas in writing?

10. Do you seek many ideas, rather than becoming satisfied with one or a few?

11. Do you know how to simplify and organize your impressions?

Your quotient is high if you can answer yes to at least eight of the eleven queries. The innovator of change, particularly in methods, needs great tenacity of purpose and stubborn resistance to discouragement. He needs initiative, curiosity, and the ability to simplify the myriad impressions that descend upon him.

chapter ten

Influencing Effects of Methods Change

A team with responsibility for initiating methods change noted that drivers of materials-handling trucks had to return to a central point for new orders. Sometimes that meant deadheading for ten minutes back to the order giver; then, for the next assignment, perhaps returning almost to where they had been in the first place. Why not equip the trucks with two-way radios?

Such an idea ought to improve the materials-handling operation's performance and efficiency. And it did with a New York–based firm, requiring one less driver per shift and speeding up the job. But in a midwestern plant, a similar move led to nothing but trouble; the union struck in protest and settled only after a compromise that offset most of the benefits of the radios.

ORGANIZING FOR METHODS CHANGE

Why the different results despite similarities, including the team approach, in both examples? Because the approach to the change in the first instance was better organized than in the second. The quality of organization is one key to influencing the effects of methods change. In the second case, no provision had been made for the union reaction to the radios. Unprepared, management acted hastily, refused to discuss the matter with employees, exacerbated the situation, and found itself facing a full-scale strike that it ended only by making compromises that probably would not have been necessary if it had better organized its approach at the beginning.

The team approach to change is a good one, but not foolproof if the team itself is poorly organized. Four guidelines help in setting up a soundly based team:

1. Top-management decision to use the team technique and willingness to give it true authority. Many companies use teams, task forces, committees, or whatever they choose to call them. But they don't give them the authority to act and enforce their decisions. In the second radio case, the team's responsibility ended after making the suggestion to install two-way radios. The plant manger took over from there, acting with little consideration for the human element. He concentrated solely on the technical aspect of getting the radios installed.

2. Definition of the team's charter. Top management should define the scope of its activity, detail the duties of the chairman, clearly state where its authority begins and ends, and indicate the length of its life. A team with a vague charter probably will accomplish few or indeterminate results because few line people will take it seriously. A charterless team with an unusually forceful chairman may show results, but perhaps at the cost of much friction or ill will from line people who see no clear authority for the team's invasion of their territory.

3. Appointment of good team members. They should all have some connection with methods changes if that is the province of the group. In the second radio case, the team was chaired by a manager of accounting, and three of the four other members were finance men. Nobody on the team had any experience with employee relations, so they could not counsel the plant manager in that area.

4. Agreement on the internal machinery for implementing the team's decisions. This differs from the guideline concerning the charter. The team in the second radio case had no device for implementing its decision. It was not supposed to get into that area. The idea was to leave implementation to the line people. This often proves weak unless the implementer was a team member to start with.

Some permanent mechanism to search out methods changes usually proves essential. That's why a unit such as a team with the specific charter to find ways for such shifts can pay off. If methods change is left solely to managers as just one aspect of their job, not too much may result because managers can only look at their own areas of responsibility, because they may be too close to see opportunities, and because they often may have a vested interest in no change.

Of course, managers can and should be on the lookout for the chance to change. The team can supplement and spur their activities.

Besides that advantage, the team can give you many others in organizing to influence the effects of methods change. Of these, three stand out:

First is unity of purpose. The team can test theories, gather knowledge about cultural patterns, and explore all facets of the situation. In the second radio case, the team failed to achieve unity because it had nothing to do with implementing the change, a fatal defect in the organization arrangements there.

Second, and perhaps most important, the team can spark teamwork, an essential in influencing change. Benjamin Fairless, when he was chairman of the United States Steel Corporation, grew impatient at the conference he was chairing because of the heated debate among several conferees. As he sat listening, he bent three paper clips into approximately straight pieces of wire. He twisted the end of each straighened piece to form one longer strand of wire. He then took three normally fashioned paper clips and strung them together into a kind of "daisy" chain. The arguers suddenly stopped their dispute as they became aware of the chairman's unaccustomed activity. Fairless, still saying nothing, pulled at the three twisted-together pieces of wire, which easily came apart. He then pulled at the three paper clips which held firm in the daisy chain. "We can't hang together like this daisy chain of paper clips," he said, "because we've become like these other three useless pieces of wire. We've lost our form—our purpose—as have these straightened paper clips." Once a team irons out any internal difficulties, it can foster teamwork in the areas of its investigation. It can win cooperation among the several functions that usually find themselves involved in any methods change. It can act as impartial arbitrator in disputes that commonly arise. It can referee in the gamesmanship that often develops during methods changes. (We'll have much more to say about this troublesome aspect of change management in the next two sections of this book.)

Third, the team can help you live with the almost-constant methods changes turning up in the 1970s in many companies, especially in medium and large companies. So numerous are such shifts that they should be monitored, and a special team can best perform this function.

SELLING THE METHODS CHANGE

The team can perform still another function—to help sell the change—which leads us to the second general method of influencing the effects of methods shifts.

The team is especially useful here because it will have several members who can all do the job of persuasion. We'll have much more to say in Chapters 17 and 18 about the need to communicate about change and to persuade others to accept it, essentially a matter of personal communication.

But now we can emphasize that the change must respond to a correctly defined need, to facilitate its "sale." A magazine called for a 10 per cent overage on its press run because of a "loss" on each issue—copies that went astray in the mails, etc. Once a year, overage stocks of each issue in storage were checked, and a clerk ordered all but 500 copies destroyed. But when the blinders were off, it was seen that the mail lists were chronically out of date. The distribution was so slow that some recipients ordered duplicate copies and never said anything about the double order. The solution was not to print 10 per cent more copies than needed, but to improve the lists and distribution system.

A related requirement in persuasion is to define the most significant feature of the change. Take time to study thoroughly the strategy of the situation. The company in the first radio case took three months to institute the change. The second company tried to jam it through in one-third that time.

High credibility helps sell methods changes, so guard it. Pay particular attention to these questions:

■ Do you explain the change fully?

■ Are you consistent in your claims for the change?

■ Have you been careful not to exaggerate claims?

■ Do you frankly report all the implications you can see in the change?

■ Do you explain promptly apparent inconsistencies in your claims?

■ Do you admit weaknesses in the proposal, along with plans to remedy them?

■ Do you have answers to opponents' arguments against your idea?

■ Will you discuss your idea fully, holding silent only on proprietary matters?

If you can answer these questions affirmatively, your credibility is high. You may not associate some of them with credibility, but certain aspects of this attribute go beyond just truth or falsehood. Credibility constitutes the main weapon in your arsenal of persuasion. Without it, all the preparations and skills in the world won't prove equal to persuading anyone to adopt and act upon your proposal for change.

A special problem in selling change, especially methods change, is to keep it sold. With methods particularly, it's only too easy to slip back into the former way of doing things.

Many a puzzled management has supervised the drastic revitalization of a company publication. All seems well: the pictures are sharp and well presented, the writing is crisp, the story selection purposeful—but only for a couple of issues. Then, things slip back to the old ways. Within a year, the magazine is just like it was before the changes so agonizingly effected.

Why does this phenomenon take place so frequently? Because of inertia, habit, and plain human cussedness. To guard against its occurrence, monitor the change. The team approach helps here because part of such a unit's job should be to prevent backsliding.

USING THE PARETO PRINCIPLE

A third general way to influence the effects of any change, but particularly methods shifts, lies in applying the Pareto principle. Vilfredo Pareto (1848–1923) was an Italian sociologist and economist living in Switzerland who discovered and applied the idea that in most situations a few factors influence the outcome, while a great many others prove largely irrelevant and can have little effect on the situation no matter what one does about them.

The Pareto statistical analysis revealed that 80 per cent of the results come from 20 per cent of the action. Therefore, the Pareto principle calls for you to identify the vital few as projects to deal with individually and to identify the trivial many as things to deal with as a class. Examples of where the Pareto principle applies include sales, quality control, inventory control, and safety.

More than one sales manager has discovered that it pays to concentrate on the few most profitable items in the line and that it does not pay to spend as much effort on the many less-profitable items. Good inventory control is based on the principle of developing stringent controls for the expensive items and treating the cheaper items as a class. Earnest quality control efforts will yield little unless they concentrate on the few factors which influence quality the most. In safety, the automobile, far and away, causes most of the deaths, so concentration on that vehicle makes use of the Pareto principle.

The difficulties with the Pareto principle are two. The first is identification of the vital few and trivial many. The second stems from the first—the realization that occasionally a factor is neither vital nor trivial. It's merely awkward.

To identify factors, list them in their order of importance. Often you can do this on the basis of costs, profitability, incidence of occurrence, or some other statistical measure. When you have no numbers, vote on their order of importance or devise some sort of ranking or other substitute for numbers. The vital few are usually unique and interdepartmental in character. You must go deep for solutions, and identification only begins the job.

An example lies in safety. A textile plant had a poor safety record. A team analyzed the situation and found that a crane operation caused the most serious accidents, but that a host of other mishaps occurred for a wide variety of reasons. Solution: The engineering department redesigned the crane operation and built some special signaling devices to warn employees on the floor when it was in action. The personnel department launched a psychological campaign to make employees aware of the need for safety. The engineering efforts aimed at the vital few; the campaign at the trivial many.

Sometimes elements fall into neither category, but into an awkward zone. Do the vital and trivial first; then go to the awkward zone. In the textile plant, the team discovered that some accidents had occurred because of horseplay. The horseplay-caused mishaps could not be specifically pinpointed; the instigators could not be identified; and a vague idefiniteness shrouded the whole situation. But after the crane redesign and the safety campaign, the incidence of horseplay dropped almost to nothing, and management didn't need to attack the problem directly.

PREPARING FOR THE NEXT METHODS CHANGE

Besides using the Pareto principle, selling the change, and organizing for it, you can markedly influence the effects of methods change by preparing for the next one even before the first one is completed.

Of course, this advance preparation is wise regardless of the kind of change, but it is especially useful with methods because so many occur, and they often have less earth-shaking import than other types.

In managing change, the managers should focus on the *next* one, not on the current. This is true even on the morning after the current upheaval.

Experience shows that many people involved with one change will spend an ensuing period defending it, until they may solidify into stand-patters.

This suggests that a true change manager should turn his back on many of the revolutionaries who have just succeeded. The best course is to start building toward the next change with a different group of people from those who probably are now devoting their energies to managing the current revolution. Usually, the new group will be younger, not yet involved in significant change, and looking for something new on which to build their reputation.

Lockheed's Maxwell W. Hunter II, an advocate of continuing change, advises, "To avoid the danger of developing ideas which the organization either cannot or will not implement, the new revolutions must contain, and probably should be led by, people with proven capability to make the current system work. Where will such leaders be found? Top management, as it keeps an eye on people, will realize that some of them think more basically about their work and try more aggressively to make changes for the good than others do. In this category, there may be a few people who have helped to pull off the latest revolution, consider its implementation as routine, are already bored, and would be perfectly willing to join the next group of revolutionaries. Assuming that they are men and women who already have a proven flair for making the present system run, they can become valuable leaders of the next revolution (and maybe even the next.)"

Although it may seem difficult to change teams at the height of success of the current revolutionaries, the move is not really hard to make. The next revolution will seem remote to most of the current instigators.

Furthermore, the next change should be mounted quietly at first—with emphasis on laying the groundwork, not yet on fighting the battle. For the revolutionaries of yesteryear, not involved in the upcoming shift, the emotional climate may be difficult when they realize they won't be the heroes tomorrow. Perhaps they can be salvaged by recruiting them for still newer changes, now in embryo but scheduled to be born after the *next* change.

THE MECHANICS OF INTRODUCING METHODS CHANGE

A fourth way to influence effects of methods change is the approach you select to introduce it. You can use, basically, three different ways:

■ Special staffs or teams. We have discussed this in detail already. We believe it's the best approach, for reasons already given.

■ Top-management edicts for quick but probably temporary action.

■ A general approach to managerial change, with change as part of the job.

While all these approaches have been used at various times in most companies, no single approach is best for every situation. It's vital to know which each can and cannot do.

Edicts, for example, can bring quick, transitory action. Edicts come in many forms and can cut shallow or deep. A common but seldom effective edict may be directed by top managers against themselves. Managers may tighten belts by eliminating the company jet, cutting back on club memberships, or monitoring expense accounts. The chief purpose of such edicts is psychological—to set an example for the rest of the company.

To make edicts really effective, top managers must spend time analyzing their departments' needs and opportunities and convincing line managers of the necessity for change.

Stanley E. Johnson Jr., president of Cooper Industries' Cooper Bessemer Company in Mt. Vernon, Ohio, and his top managers studied every phase of the company for nearly a month before issuing an edict. When issued, it worked because of the prior planning.

Massey-Ferguson Industries Ltd., Toronto, achieved success with the third method. Its integrated planning and control system sets profit improvement goals for each major component of the company and then forces each manager to spell out profit improvement projects each year as part of the corporate budgetary process.

In summary, the team approach gets high marks, especially when it's used with the third. The edict ranks last as approach, but it does have value if a psychological effect is the major benefit desired.

No method is foolproof, of course, and the manager of change should accept three drawbacks to making any change:

First, results usually are slow in coming, frequently taking several years before big improvements are evident. So patience is necessary.

Second, the administrative burden is unavoidable. Each technique requires much managerial time and effort which costs money. That burden must be accepted.

Third, enthusiasm must be recharged periodically.

part four

Organizations Change

chapter eleven

"The Management Announces..."

"The management announces that, effective————, our organizational structure will be realigned to reflect changes among those we serve and to take greater advantage of growing capabilities of employees . . . !"

How many people have read or heard at least once during their working lives an announcement of an organizational change which began something like the foregoing? Most have encountered it more than once and may bear the mental or psychological scars to remind them of it.

In a recent thirty-six-month period, 66 major corporations of 100 surveyed announced significant organizational changes. A major restructuring about every two years is probably average for most medium and large operations. Why all the shakeups? Two reasons probably are those stated in the typical reorganizational announcement cited above—changes in markets and in the work force. A third reason is to make more change more possible elsewhere in the operation. One research study shows that 90 per cent of the executives surveyed believe that overly rigid organizational factors work against change elsewhere in the operation— 12 per cent said this was a serious factor, 38 per cent said it was fairly serious, 40 per cent said it was not too serious but still a problem, and 10 per cent believed it was no problem.

The study reveals that middle- and lower-level managers, particularly, are skeptical about a corporation's organizational ability to change. The overwhelming majority do not believe themselves personally challenged to do anything particularly new or different.

Yet a wide range of managers believe that an operation cannot survive without change. Samples:

■ "Companies that take refuge behind the rock of security find that it soon becomes their tombstone."—David Rockefeller, chairman of Chase Manhattan Bank.

■ "In business and industry, change is the price of health and vigor, and eventually even of survival."—David H. Dawson, vice president of Du Pont.

■ "The great challenge to management today is to recognize and to respond effectively to the accelerating tempo of change that characterizes our society and economy."—Orville E. Beal, president of Prudential Insurance.

Top managers who believe this—and a majority probably does—often start with organizational change because it's close at hand, it serves as a symbol and example, and it really may accomplish what the press releases and employee announcements claim for it.

The greatest problem with organizational change is that it too often is done chiefly or only for reasons of symbolism and show. This and the next two chapters will deal with how to make organizational change for the right reasons.

WHAT IS AN ORGANIZATION?

It's an engine to maximize human resources. It divides the work and provides the means of coordinating it. Organizational theorists, in general, take two views on how to accomplish this—the classical approach and the behavioral-science approach. The first is rather rigid and formal. The second holds that the organization should be flexible according to the people involved in the various jobs.

During the 1950s and early 1960s, business courses in organizational development customarily set forth descriptions of various types of structures, such as these:

- Functional (by marketing, manufacturing, etc.)
- Divisional (by product, region, customer, etc.)
- Line and staff
- Hierarchical chain of command

In the first two types, both the classical and the behavioral approach can be applied. In the third type, both can still be applied, but the classical more easily than the behavioral. In the fourth type, only the classical applies for all practical purposes.

Classroom activities in the 1950s and early 1960s focused on learning the mechanics of each type. Although courses and textbooks recognized that each kind of organization could apply to different situations, the process of adapting structures to the needs of the situation receive only modest attention.

In this same period, businesses themselves often made a religion out of formal organization charts and traditional organizational setups. Many observers have charged that some planners tried to force real work groupings to fit the chart, rather than to develop structure that matched actual operations.

Yet deep changes have been taking place in business organization itself. For instance, some firms have grappled with introducing product management, which doesn't fit well into traditional patterns, while others have hunted for better ways to integrate their divisionalized operations.

Many companies discovered that traditional methods, particularly the formalized style, didn't provide them with structures adequate to such problems. The formal style, especially, with rigid divisions of responsibility and authority and mechanistic chains of command, proved too inflexible to meet many of the needs of the changing 1960s and 1970s.

So industry needed a new look at organizational development. Theorists tried to meet the demand with a whole range of suggested approaches. One is the "contingency" theory of organization. Its main point is that there is no "one best way" to organize, but that different companies in different industries need different kinds of structures at various stages of their growth.

Where the industry technology is stable and predictable (as in the container industry), a traditional, pyramidal organization may be best. Where the industry technology is unpredictable and the products diverse (as in plastics), a decentralized, nonhierarchical organization may be best.

Two proponents of this approach, Paul R. Lawrence and Jay W. Lorsch (in their book *Organization and Environment,* Richard D. Irwin, Inc., 1969), advise managers of organizational change to examine and categorize different types of organizational needs, different stages of a company's growth, different kinds of environments, etc., and then to identify organizational structures that might serve best in each situation.

With this approach, it is unproductive to study the mechanics of different types of traditional structures only, because changing business requirements often must be met with new and different types of structures—some of which may be unknown today and many of which will be unique to the company developing them. Under this theory, managers of organizational change must learn to analyze situations and develop approaches which uniquely meet the new needs. They must shift from developing formal charts and traditional structures to developing individualized and adaptive arrangements that meet requirements of their particular industries.

Going a step further than the "contingency" theory is what Robert J. Mockler calls the "situational" theory.[1] The professor of management at St. John's University, New York, says the emphasis of situational organization shifts from the universal guideline to the study of such situations as operating requirements, individual and work-group needs, and the leadership style of individual supervisors.

The emergence of the situational approach results from an attempt to reorient management theory towards management practice, not from any attempt to shuffle management theory. The situational approach starts with a manager who works in a specific job situation and who recognizes that he must adapt any theory to meet his actual needs. Theory conflicts result from the job situation. For instance, if the work situation requires reconciling behavioral and business needs, the manager looks at both the human and business aspects, determines the impact of each, and balances any conflicting needs in choosing and instituting his organizational solution. He will look at both the behavioral and formal schools of planning for his answers.

The situational approach brings reality to organizational planning. "Too many theorists," says Mockler, "in the past have tended to develop oversimplified general theories and so have lost touch with the realities of the actual management job. The approach also discourages the study of different areas of management theory as ends in themselves, and leads instead to studying the ways in which different management theories and methods can work together in helping a manager do his job."

Basically, the situational approach involves these steps:

■ Diagnose the situation to define basic problems and parameters, to clarify management objectives, and to identify a solution.

[1] *Harvard Business Review*, May–June 1971, Copyright 1971 by the President and Fellows of Harvard University.

- Study the facts to isolate the key factors affecting decision making.
- Develop alternative courses of action.
- Evaluate each alternative to determine which one best meets the situation's specific needs.
- Convert the decision into action.

How might this situational technique work out? Take the case of a diversified company which has both unionized and nonunionized operations. Its personnel department was organized along conventional lines—compensation, benefits, employee practices, contract negotiating, and communication specialists. In practice, the department tended to focus more on the unionized than on the nonunionized elements of the employee population because this was where the publicized difficulties lay and where the short-term penalties—such as strikes—were most likely to occur in case of failure.

For years, management talked about the need to focus more attention on nonunionized employees, but no particularly different action resulted from the talk. Finally, management reorganized the personnel function—setting up one section to concentrate on the unionized portion of the employee population and another to deal with the nonunionized. The change required a few more people, but the company for the first time gave needed and effective attention to the employees who weren't organized. The improved operation far more than offset the added expense of the department.

Sometimes organizational shortcomings that would seem obvious aren't obvious to the people involved and can lead to far-reaching troubles. One company decided to move its corporate headquarters out of a midwestern city to a nearby suburb. It assigned a corporate vice-president with overall responsibility for the design and construction of the new headquarters building and the general planning of the move. The executive, who normally had responsibility for long-term company planning, headed a small staff. So he was authorized to go to other departments for help on the special project.

Being a professional planner, the vice-president considered all the contingencies—if a snag in the zoning of the suburban property should come to light, if a civil-rights group or a clerical union should protest the move out of the city, if a suburban homeowner group in the new location should oppose the arrival. He borrowed company lawyers, public relations men, and personnel men to prepare contingency plans in case anything of this sort developed. The paperwork generated necessitated the hiring of four secretaries from a temporary-help agency. Parkinson's law came into play with a vengeance; only when the managers of those company experts who had been borrowed for the project began to protest did the president call a halt.

The problem here was that there was no organizational structure. The vice-president built it as he went along, and it grew like Topsy. The structure needs to be planned. It just can't be allowed to evolve. Casual evolution will produce casual or worse results. Changes in organization can of course come, but they must be planned. In the next two chapters we will deal with how to plan wisely. For the rest of this one, we will explore the benefits of planned organizational change and the characteristics of a good structure that maximizes human resources.

BENEFITS FROM GOOD ORGANIZATIONAL CHANGE

You change your organization for many good reasons, but these four stand out:

1. *To operate more effectively.* More work can be done at less cost when the structure has been designed in accordance with sound, proven principles. The structure itself becomes the logical framework that lets more individuals know what is expected of them, why and when it needs to get done, and what it should cost.

2. *To achieve balanced growth.* By giving balanced attention to the future, today's work will not tend to get done at the expense of tomorrow's. A well-planned structure separates present responsibilities from development work and plans for the proper balance.

3. *To keep up with the times.* Stated another way, this means to avoid becoming obsolete. A well-planned structure encourages coupling new technology to work now being done, and does this with a minimum of disruption. Good organizational planning helps prevent the crisis of unforeseen unemployment on the one hand and the sudden shortage of some specialized talent on the other.

4. *To be more flexible.* Good planning tries to achieve a balance between making things happen and allowing things to happen. When people are unaware of the scope of their own and others' jobs, they probably won't take advantage of unanticipated opportunities. They also won't react quickly or at all to unforeseen problems. Both situations get resolved more rapidly when everyone knows what is expected of him and also what to expect from others.

CHARACTERISTICS OF A GOOD ORGANIZATION

When you change an organization, the change should aim at one or more of the four preceding benefits. The change should also embody all six of the following characteristics:

First, the structure needs to be *logical*. It needs to make sense to those who must work within its framework. As an example, in a mature organization where people have worked together for some time, it would be possible to put apprentice tool-and-die training under the manager of finance and things would move along for a while without immediate difficulty. People have an uncanny way of making almost any setup work.

Soon, though, both the manager of apprentice training and the apprentices themselves would be spending a lot of time justifying to others why they happen to be within the finance part of the organization. And the background of the finance manager hardly puts him in a good position to evaluate the effectiveness of apprentice training, to help in its planning, to set budgets, or to hire and motivate an apprentice-training director.

This example is absurd, of course, but the lack of logic in the arrangement is apparent. There are many other instances, however, where organizational choices may not be so clear. Even in such cases, the final logic of the structure needs to be apparent to those who work within it. The best design is one whose logic leaps at you when you first encounter it.

For instance, it's easy for an advertising copy writer, a point-of-purchase display designer, a direct-mail specialist, and a catalog editor to see how their jobs contribute to the effectiveness of a sales-promotion component. Similarly, the logic is apparent in combining components for sales promotion, field sales, marketing research, and product planning in one marketing component. They all contribute to marketing objectives. Marketing, engineering, manufacturing, relations, finance, and legal components then get their common identification through the continuing objectives and current goals of the overall business. The various groupings and relationships have a logic that is readily apparent.

A related characteristic of a well-planned structure is that it be *understandable*. To the extent that it is clear, simple, and relatively uncomplicated, it will be readily communicated and readily understood. The more complex the relationships, the more difficult it will be to get the needed understanding, acceptance, and use. It's hard enough for most people to stay ahead of all the other things they have to know about a business without having to learn the details of an involved and intricate structure.

The best arrangement will also be *explicit*. Anticipate and avoid potential ambiguity in terms and relationships. For instance, responsibilities that are essentially territorial shouldn't be assigned in terms of cities. What territory is covered by the New York office? Rather, define the geographic limits of responsibilities for such a position in terms of the actual counties, states or other areas served.

A fourth characteristic of a good structure: design it in accordance with sound, proven *principles*. Such principles include:

■ Each individual should report to one and only one manager.

■ Spans of managerial responsibility ought to be selected in accordance with the kind of work and the interrelationship of positions being managed.

■ Levels in the structure should be as few as possible, consistent with well-designed spans of responsibility.

■ Positions should be designed in terms of responsibility for specific, measurable results, with each position as far as possible responsible for completed work.

■ Jobs ought to be designed for maximum use of self-measurement, with feedback of results going first to the individuals doing the work.

■ Assistants, coordinators, and other roving positions with unclear responsibilities should be eliminated.

■ Open communications channels, with a liberal flow of information on a need-to-know basis, ought to be part of the structure.

In applying such principles, the designer of an organization needs to strike a balance between *flexibility* and *stability*.

Assignments of responsibility need to be sufficiently durable that individuals can get to know their work and their work relationships. In some businesses, this may be difficult. In the defense areas in particular, where contracts get discontinued and whole programs are subject to the voting vicissitudes of congressional committees, many technical people find it difficult to stay in one spot long enough to learn their work well. Experience in such areas has proved again and again how disruptive and unproductive is the climate when work assignments are changed too frequently.

It takes time to learn, understand, and use productively the many work relationships in any position. For instance, among the more complicated work relationships in General Electric are those defining various responsibilities of pooled selling components. The Power Generation Sales Division, for example, is a field selling organization handling the sale of products to electric utilities throughout the country. This pooled selling component handles field sales for the products of many different product departments. Marketing planning and pricing strategies, however, are the assigned responsibilities of the department general manager and the marketing manager in each business.

The work relationships of a sales engineer in field sales take time to learn and to handle smoothly. He will be calling on an electric utility handling the products of several different departments. He needs to learn to whom to look for information and assistance in each of the departments whose products he handles. A volatile, changing structure will not make his business life any easier.

The organization also needs to be sufficiently stable for individuals to plan their business careers for reasonable lengths of time. To be sure, in an environment of accelerating change, this becomes more difficult every year. Yet most people like to make at least some plans for the future—for themselves, for their family, and for the education and recreation of their children. Capricious changes in work assignments do not help in personal planning.

Stability of the organization also enables employees to carry on in a consistent manner if for any reason the manager or general manager is suddenly removed. This may be through death, transfer, retirement, or illness. A well-understood, reasonably stable structure is the framework within which people carry on during the transition to a new leader.

On the other hand, the structure needs to be sufficiently flexible to motivate people to meet unanticipated problems and take advantage of unforeseen opportunities.

Flexibility in the assignment of work made it possible for General Electric to capitalize on such opportunities as the gas turbine and Man-Made diamonds. In both instances, there was very little standing on ceremony or adhering to past precedent when the time came to introduce the products. Determining which plant should make them and which organizational components should take them to market was done on the basis of what made sense to the business, not to preserve a rigid structure.

The diamond business originated in the Research Laboratory, went through the pilot stage and on into production. The concept actually moved through several different components before being established on its own as the Specialty Materials Business Department.

Of course, when your own job is at stake, you may be somewhat less enthusiastic about flexibility in organizational structure. But technologies change, markets change and jobs have to change, too. If they don't a business will find its setup isn't the only thing that's out of date. The whole show may go down the drain.

One way to relieve the individual's anxiety is to build a record of smoothly executed changes. Jobs, components, and work relationships get changed to meet competitive pressures, to take advantage of innovation, or to pursue new markets. But when managers and other employees know from having been treated fairly that they will continue to be treated fairly—that they will get a chance to participate and they will be kept informed—then change becomes a way of business life and is not feared. (More on this in Part Five.)

Most people who have moved through organizational changes smoothly and without undue anxiety know that such shifts usually mean more opportunity, not less. When they feel this way, they will be motivated toward business goals.

There is one final test of a good structure, one ultimate screen for all work. All work must *add value*—value that some customer is willing to pay for. The cost of every task, every position, every piece of work in a business must be recovered in the price charged to some customer for a product or service.

This seems so self-evident that it's hardly worth repeating. But it all too frequently is ignored when planning changes or additions in positions and organizational components. Basically, it is the test for work that distinguishes the nice from the necessary. Nice work may be fun to have around in lush times. But only the necessary work adds more value than it costs, and the value it adds is value that customers can see.

The criterion of added value is especially brutal in testing the need for staff work, for special assistants, for study teams, for coordinators, for pooled purchasing and other work pools. Admittedly for such work the link between contribution and customers is long and indistinct. But the discipline of seeking the justification for work through this link is worth the effort. Constant questioning of work in terms of the cost/value relationship is vitally necessary to keep a business competitive.

chapter twelve

Getting Set
for Organization Change

The plant manager of a Midwestern manufacturer called a dinner meeting. Those attending sat at round tables on a strictly departmental basis. The manager dined in solitary splendor at a
table in the middle of the room.

After the dinner, the manager reviewed the objectives of the
operation for the year and pointed out that, sitting as they were
in departmental isolation, they really couldn't come to grips with
the problems. Then he moved the meeting into the next room,
which had been set up on an interdepartmental basis so that people could communicate easily with each other. As the discussion
progressed, the interdependence of the departments became clear,
making it possible for the manager to emphasize that "the only
way we can meet our goals and solve our problems is to break

down organizational barriers and use the knowledge of all the people around us."

WHEN THE ORGANIZATION
NEEDS TO CHANGE

In effect, he served notice that the organization's structure would be changed if barriers remained high between departments. Poor communication constitutes one important indicator that organizational change is needed. We'll deal with this in greater detail in the final part of the book. Now we'll concentrate on seven other clues, among many, that signal the need for possible shifts in your structure for maximizing human efforts.

1. Ineffective Operations

Missed production schedules, numerous other snafus, and conflicting or overlapping spheres of authority often signal organizational troubles. They may signal other shortcomings, such as ineffective people, but look at the organization first.

A machine tool manufacturer had two nearby plants. Each factory performed certain processes for both—all turning, drilling, etc., was done in one, and all sheet-metal work in the other. Although the same works manager supervised production in both, each factory had its own production controller. The production controller in factory B decided that the stock levels of a number of parts for his products were too low, and he raised the minimum stock figures on the inventory cards. Orders for making these parts in numbers sufficient to meet these higher levels had been passed in routine fashion to the machine shop in factory A, which had consequently found its monthly output program abnormally high. Orders for metal stocks also rose later on. The pressure on his machine shop and the rise in material costs mystified production controller A, since they were not apparently related to a comparable rise in the forecast of final units to be turned out in either plant. Production controller A eventually ran the thing to earth, but at the cost of some confusion and considerable exasperation.

The solution in this case was to give the authority for production control in both plants to one man, just as the overall supervision in both was vested in one manager.

2. Unbalanced Growth

A maker of gardening tools and equipment found its hand-tool business growing well, while the power-tool phase of its operation lagged. This proved especially puzzling because market surveys showed that competitors were experiencing just the opposite results. Investigation turned up a clue to the trouble. Hand tools were marketed through hardware distributors; power tools through manufacturers' agents. The distributors usually served a small geographical area, a city or county. But the agents covered several states. Power tools weren't getting as much sales attention as hand tools.

The solution: Persuade the distributors to take on the power tools as well as the hand items wherever possible, but especially in suburban areas. The change in the sales organization solved the problem of unbalanced growth within a year.

Unbalanced growth may surface anywhere—in product lines, in engineering service, in any other aspect of the business. It's a sign that your organization needs changing.

3. Obsolescence

A buggy-whip manufacturer needs more than a new organization to put himself to rights. He needs a new product—accelerator pedals, perhaps. But the organization of the former buggy-whip maker may need dramatic change when he turns out accelerators.

Until 1960, Reynolds Metals Company had a difficult time persuading food packers that their approach to metal cans was obsolete. Partly, this turned out to be an organizational problem. Reynolds persuaded Minute Maid Company to install a machine at its Auburndale, Florida, plant for in-plant aluminum can assembly. Thus twin new concepts for the Florida citrus industry were born: commercial use of aluminum cans and in-plant assembly of cans.

Why didn't the can companies, themselves, introduce this concept? Because they were focused on the organizational concept of production integration, largely from tinplate. They made their cans in their own plants, then shipped them to the food-packing customers. For a time, they suffered organizational obsolescence, which delayed them in turning to aluminum and to producing in the customer's plant.

Every new product probably calls for some shifts in your organization. Every new key man in your organization may require organizational shifts, too, because people should not be forced into the mold of an organization. The organization should fit the people involved. Even when the products don't change, and the people running the operation remain the same, the structure may need refurbishing in time because the market changes or the individuals age.

A maker of detachable collars for men's shirts still makes the same product, and a few of the key people of the 1920s still are around today. But the organization has changed mightily because the market has changed from a general haberdashery item to a specialized product—paper collars for waiters, bell-hops, and doormen.

Obsolescence takes many forms, and it's inevitable eventually. Therefore, organizational change is inevitable eventually.

4. Inflexibility

Inflexibility often accounts for a company's failure to recognize obsolescence. But how do you recognize your own organizational inflexibility? Among many symptoms, these stand out:

■ When you haven't changed in two years or more. This doesn't mean that you need to change, but it is time to examine your organization for the possibility of change.

■ When you find various supervisors in your operation refusing assignments on the ground that "It isn't in my charter," or "I thought Ed's component handled that," or "We're badly overloaded now—we'll do it next month."

■ When some people are truly overloaded but others don't have enough to do. Then your manning tables, a factor in organization, are inflexible.

■ When good people leave you for vague or "better opportunity elsewhere" reasons. If a man can't get ahead in your organization, there may be something wrong with the setup.

■ When you suffer from any or all of the three previously mentioned symptoms—ineffective operations, unbalanced growth, or obsolescence.

5. Vague or Conflicting Goals

This proves to be an almost invariable indication of organizational trouble. A characteristic which shows up most frequently in successful business is the knowledge generally held of where the business is going. Most of the decision makers know what the plans are, what results are expected, what strategies they should follow to achieve the results. Also, they know that they can make decisions readily and that their decisions will be in general harmony with desired results. As a corollary, if you don't communicate business objectives, they might as well not exist. With unknown goals or with conflicting aims, people tend not to know their jobs and responsibilities. Of course, they don't accept plans and responsibilities if they don't know what they are. In the case of conflicting objectives, the situation may prove even worse. That can lead to rival factions, in which no organization can survive. A business or operation has room in its setup for only one set of objectives, strategies, and plans at a time.

Some companies have experienced trouble in hiring more blacks partly because the responsibility for integrating the work force is diffused. In a midwestern plant, the personnel department believed integration was part of its charter, but much of its action got countermanded or dissipated by a newly formed department of urban affairs, which reported directly to the company president, whereas the personnel people had much lower reporting status, to the plant manager. The two components accomplished little but mutual frustration until the personnel manager, with the plant manager's support, went to the president and demanded a solution.

The plant manager didn't win a higher reporting status, but he did get understanding that he, not the urban affairs manager, had sole responsibility for hiring blacks.

6. Lack of Tempo

If you cannot take the position that most of your decisions are made and implemented as if the survival of your business depended on it, you probably have a tempo—and an organizational—problem. Apply this survival test. If you find that many things would have been accomplished much faster had survival been the issue, then your organization runs at too slow a pace.

This does not mean that long hours are the issue. On the contrary, working long hours more likely indicates poor tempo and bad organization. When the organization and tempo are right, people can shorten their work week by eliminating the fiddling around, the frantic haste, the useless work, or the dedicated procrastination.

Check yourself and your key people with the next half-dozen decisions you make or are involved in. Could they as easily have been made in half the time and could the schedule for their implementation just as easily have been half as long?

A pyramidal structure with many levels of management, reporting, and approval may serve some purposes, but certainly not speed.

An organizational study of the Post Office revealed this as one of the problems of the old U.S. department. Under the new semipublic setup, a major objective was to streamline the organization to speed decision making.

7. Incapacity for Renewal

Organizations parallel people, animals, and plants, in that they have a life cycle running from youth to old age. But unlike people, animals, and plants, they should have the capacity for gradual renewal. Good organizations change continually, although usually in small ways. A minor realignment of duties may occur one month in a good organization, a change in title a couple of months later, a new man may assume a key job six months after that. If these little changes don't or can't occur, you need to change your organization so that they can. Otherwise, it will decay.

A veteran sales manager suffered a heart attack and died six months later. His replacement, who also served as acting manager during his illness, was the second in command. The department went through the transition with scarcely a ripple. The deceased and the new managers had worked smoothly in tandem for years.

Little really changed—except the sales curve, which began to drop. What happened? The same sales methods continued. The product remained about the same. Competitive conditions showed no drastic differences.

Eventually, the new manager departed, and the department went through a drastic overhaul. A survivor commented, "It was strange. With the new man we expected change, but nothing happened. We got stale, bored. His arrival made us realize we were in a rut; suddenly it hit us that nothing new had happened in a long time."

This problem is not quite one of inflexibility, the fourth symptom. It is more one of stagnation. One way to avoid such decay lies in an organization that provides a hospitable environment for the individual. People made to feel like cogs in a machine will probably behave like cogs. They won't produce ideas for change. They will probably resist such ideas when suggested by others.

WHEN THE ORGANIZATION
NEEDS NO CHANGE

While our thesis is that often the organization needs to change, sometimes it's incorrectly pinpointed as the source of ills. An iatrogenic phenomenon in medicine occurs when a doctor's actions or words induce an illness in a patient. A similar malady may occur in your operation if you fuss with your organizational structure when you should look elsewhere for remedies. In so doing, you may end up with real organizational problems.

No clearcut guides exist to know whether you are flirting with "iatrogenics," but here are typical examples of where it has occurred:

■ Some conglomerate managements or new bosses almost routinely reorganize a recent acquisition or a new operation. Yet the new unit may stay sick because its product or its financing, not its organization, may be ailing.

■ Certain ills, such as poor creativity, may be laid to poor organization. That's seldom the cause. Management is more often the culprit, as implied in the cartoon showing two people lying on a couch, with one saying, "Tomorrow we've got to get organized." Another instance: unprofitable operations. The organization doesn't dictate that they continue, but management does.

■ Some managers change for the sake of change alone. But if the change won't improve operations, help achieve a balanced growth, forestall obsolescence, or improve flexibility, there's no good reason for it. Odds are that such a change will do more harm than good.

■ The organization often gets confused with the manager. The structure may be sound, but the manager weak. Yet the attention goes to the former rather than the latter.

Any operation with effective measurements, such as the discipline of the market, lessens the danger that it will make unnecessary organizational shifts. This explains why a business organization suffers less often from "iatrogenics" than does government. Business must face almost daily the discipline of the market. Government must face only the discipline of the public, which is largely unorganized, often voiceless except at election time, and —worst of all—frequently indifferent.

WHY ORGANIZATIONAL CHANGE IS ESPECIALLY DIFFICULT

When you change an organization, you often have two organizations to shift—the formal and the informal. The bigger the organization, the more likely it is that a sub-rosa setup has gradually grown in and around and under the formal setup.

■ Two managers are incompatible, so they have evolved various bypassing arrangements whereby their tangential work can somehow get accomplished.

■ One manager finds that approvals come slowly from a higher group that must pass on some aspects of his work. So he works out ingenious devices to get approvals from a more compatible manager whose status parallels that of the other group.

■ A sales manager doesn't go through channels to get a design change for a special customer, but goes directly to the design engineer, a close personal friend.

The list of expedient methods could go on and on. The point is that you must deal with them when you manage organizational change. First, you must be aware that they exist, how they work, and why they work. Your new organizational design should take into account their good features and provide for safeguards to prevent the bad features from developing in a clandestine way again. Incidentally, many organizational changes really formalize much of the informal arrangements. Finally, you must make sure that, as you get set for the change, you are aware of the psychological hazards of that task, in shifting both the informal and formal structures.

Past success tends to get monumentalized in the present because policies and attitudes which led to that success are overvalued. As long as the environment and competition remain static, such policies and attitudes help stabilize the operation.

But environment and competition seldom stay static for long. Then the policies and attitudes, which have become part of a system of beliefs, traditions, habits, and inhibitions in the operation, inhibit change. That's why, paradoxically, past success makes present change much more difficult than past failure in an organization.

This phenomenon works more insidiously in this area of organizational change than in any other. Culture plays a more powerful role in the organization than it does in technology or among individual people. An organization that has been successful develops a culture as distinctive as the cultural differences between nations or the personality differences between individuals. National cultures, individual personalities, and organizational cultures don't change readily.

So the organization must avoid becoming the prisoner of its own past success. Many members of the successful organization see the threat to change it as an attack at the least or treason at the worst.

This explains why, when two comparable organizations merge, painful adjustments almost invariably follow as the differences in corporate style and culture get resolved. The same holds when a new man from outside the organization takes over.

You probably cannot avoid all these problems of change. All organizations must adapt to changes in the climate around them, or die. If put under enough pressure, all organizations can change. Yet, this pressure must either be external or the result of strong internal leadership.

Not often does any organization generate sufficient pressure internally from the ranks to produce important directional changes. Why? Because the internally produced change is tantamount to expressing dissatisfaction with the organization's leaders. Good leaders themselves, however, can accomplish such internal and evolutionary change when they actively guide it and explicitly direct it.

Yet they face large dilemmas. The organization has made a heavy investment in the status quo. Changes are inherently threatening, leading to a chain reaction of shifts in objectives, values, status, and hierarchy and putting many cherished beliefs in jeopardy.

Many members of an organization don't have the opportunity to see the needs for change until well after the optimum time for action has passed. Corporate culture blinds these people to the need for change until the overwhelming majority in it can accept the need for change. When that requirement becomes so obvious, you have lost the competitive advantage in flexibility and speed.

On the other hand, a manager who early sees the need for change and tries to do something about it may endanger his own ability to lead. He needs courage as well as skill to put the change across in the face of almost certain, if subliminal, opposition.

Major organizational changes should and usually do lead to an attitude of caution and conservatism. Those attitudes won't budge until the instigator of change can communicate both the reasons for the change and their probable consequences. He'll have trouble with the latter because any significant change produces a train of interrelated and perhaps unanticipated follow-on changes.

Thus the manager of organizational change, particularly in the case of an organization that has enjoyed success in the past, assumes considerable personal risk. He asks that the apparent verities of the past successes be abandoned for unproven changes based upon uncertain data. And, to the risk of failure from incorrect choice, add the risk of failure in leadership because most members of the organization don't recognize the need for the change. Even the best-chosen risks may still prove fatal to the current leadership if the consequences are unprovable in fact.

So should you avoid organizational change if at all possible? No, but you should be aware of the risks and willing to accept the penalty of failure. The rewards can be substantial, even enormous, if the effort is successful.

One large company revamped the organization that had responsibility for introducing new products. The new organization changed the procedures. The storm arose over the new procedures, not the organization as such responsible for them.

The critics failed to see what was wrong with the former methods; they objected to streamlining measures as weakening control; they criticized the new appraisal and testing techniques.

Top management stuck by the new organization. Gradually, opinion began swinging more toward the new procedures. One new product introduced by the new organization became a success; the criticism disappeared. Not so incidently, the manager of the organization which had engineered the new product introduction change eventually became the firm's vice-president of development.

How easily the story could have had a different ending. The introduction techniques could have flopped, and the organization with it.

A manager involved in organizational change must meet three requirements to achieve it:

1. Conceive and make explicit a superior organization.
2. Provide the leadership necessary to overcome the obstacles to changing the existing structure.
3. Provide the leadership at a time when the organization as a whole would probably oppose the changes needed.

chapter thirteen

Making Organizational Change Work for You

When United States Steel Corporation announced a sweeping re-organization, it gave more than three months' notice, and management from the chairman on down emphasized this point: "The corporation will make every effort to accomplish this transition with full consideration for the human values involved."

Behind this announcement lay much thought, effort, and study on what to change, how to implement that change, and where to control it so that the reorganization would bring maximum benefit to the steel corporation and its employees. The "what," "how," and "where" are three legs of the stool that can support successful organizational change. Let's examine each of the basics in detail.

WHAT TO CHANGE

Nobody but you can determine what you should reorganize; restructuring should be tailored to your needs and objectives.

So careful study of those requirements and aims is the first step in knowing what to change. Your next step is to apply the alternative proposals of change to see how well they would embody the six characteristics of a good organization described in Chapter 11—as to whether the proposed change is logical, understandable, explicit, based on sound organizational principles, capable of flexibility, and capable of adding value to the work.

Take the case of a large company that wants to get into some promising new markets or technologies. The conventional organizational approach would be—and usually is—to set up a new operation within the company to exploit the opportunity. But dozens of alert big companies—Alcoa, Boise Cascade, Coca-Cola, Dow Chemical, Du Pont, Ford, General Electric, International Paper, Mobil Oil, Singer, Standard Oil (N.J.), and Union Carbide among them—have taken a different organizational approach. Several have established wholly owned subsidiaries. Such an organization provides venture capital to help small companies to "grow." Under typical arrangements, its investments in each may run up to about 45 per cent.

The president of one says: "We are designed to implement our parent company's growth through the development of new businesses. We invest in small firms, work with them through their formative years, and eventually work toward merging them with appropriate operating components."

Consequently, one of the three general criteria such an organization considers in searching for investment opportunities is a "fit" with some existing or planned future business in the parent. A second and related criterion is that the company's management is amenable to a working relationship with the parent. A third is that the firm meet acceptable standards of growth prospects, return on investment, etc.

Areas of investment for one such organization include fields of high technology where it seems preferable to implement the parent's growth externally rather than through internal developments. Among these fields are communications, environment, industrial and consumer services, automation, medical and industrial instrumentation, microelectronics, and esoteric materials.

Such wholly owned subsidiaries can make this kind of organizational change work because parent company managers diagnosed the problem, studied the facts, developed and evaluated alternatives to meet the diagnosis and facts, and converted the evaluation into action.

When you go through this exercise, you may also spot what not to change. Many existing organizational arrangements have latent pluses that you should not overlook. For instance, consider the much-maligned meeting.

To improve efficiency and to save time, one company substituted conference calls for meetings. Surprisingly, this minor organizational shift met with a poor reception. Meetings served valued latent functions. They enabled informal, casual conversations that every organization seems to need. These requirements weren't met with conference calls. The company returned to the face-to-face meetings.

When changes are made on the obvious level without an equal awareness of the potential latent disruptions, strains may arise that even the organization itself may not fully understand. And often these strains get projected in the form of extraneous or misleading issues that impede the management of change.

Knowing what to change may involve going to temporary organizational arrangements, sometimes called "adhocracy." Short-term organizations can handle a specific problem, such as the introduction of a new product or the building of a new plant. When the problem is solved, the organization is disbanded.

Or the organization may be permanent, but its focus changing as circumstances dictate. This may happen in organizations charged with plant security, for example. In the early 1960s before the advent of student activists and radical-left elements, the security force was a preventive unit to guard against the conventional threats of fire, theft, and vandalism. But the rise of mob action in the late 1960s and early 1970s necessitated an entirely different and more positive organization to cope with confrontations, bombs, and other sabotage, in addition to the more customary dangers.

And finally, consider the organization which must resight its goals to match the changing concerns of the public. Public-affairs or urban-orientation components face these challenges. They must take into account relativism—the balancing of the traditional goals of profits and costs against new ones such as needs for individual satisfactions, group norms, and social causes.

But, to repeat, only you can design your own organization. It can't be lifted bodily from a manual; it must be tailor-made.

HOW TO CHANGE

When you know what to change in the organization, you next must know how to change it. While the following rules apply to making any change, they are particularly pertinent for organizational change with its unusually strong cultural barriers to any shifts (as discussed in Chapter 12):

1. Explain why. Provide all the facts about the reason for changing. If there are risks, acknowledge them, but tell why the risk is worth taking. Show what you have done to minimize the risk. Often the organizational arrangement you have selected is itself designed to minimize risk—as in the case of the venture-capital setup.

2. Name the benefits that could result from the change. Don't exaggerate, but list them objectively. Not to do so would be like a salesman not telling a customer what his product can do for him.

3. Seek questions and answer them. This will stop rumors that inevitably arise during an organizational move. The grapevine flourishes before, during, and after the organization changes. Cut in to cut it off. (For more on the grapevine, see Chapter 17.)

4. Invite participation. Ask for suggestions on how best to reorganize, because the people involved know the situation best, and changes work out most favorably when those concerned have a part in suggesting the change.

5. Avoid surprise. This stirs unreasoning opposition more than any other factor because those involved don't have time to think. Their emotions take over, and such emotions are most likely to be negative.

6. Acknowledge the rough spots. In selling an organizational change, especially, we tend to make it sound simple, presenting a clearcut chart and neat lines of authority and responsibility. But even a minor organizational change is rarely simple. Admit it, and tell how you plan to smooth the shift.

7. Set standards. Give a date when you want the change to be completed. Tell what you want it to accomplish. People want to know what's expected. They will help achieve the standards only when and if they know what they are. Be as specific as possible about these standards. The standard, "to better utilize our existing workforce," may be all right for a press release, but it won't do for the people involved in the reorganization. They want to know how the new setup is expected to perform and by what time. What are the penalties for failure? The rewards for success? The reorganization of the employee-relations component, mentioned earlier in Chapter 11, proved successful because the goal was explicitly stated—to provide more service and attention to nonunionized employees.

8. Contact informal leaders. Every organization has somebody in the ranks who performs at least a quasi-leadership role even though he isn't formally designated as a manager. Let him know in particular detail what's going on.

9. Praise. People in any new situation, but especially a reorga-

nization, are anxious. If you can do so honestly, let them know that they are cooperating well and that progress is being made.

10. Repeat. To put over something with the ramifications common to reorganizations, you must tell the story over and over, using fresh examples and different approaches.

As you apply the foregoing ten rules for change, bear in mind that you must use them to help overcome four psychological and other roadblocks that turn up particularly often in reorganizations.

1. The need for the familiar
2. The need for order
3. The fear of risk
4. The compulsion to conform

Let's examine each in detail.

1. The Need for the Familiar

Even when we know the existing organization is bad, we tend to hang onto it because at least it is known. The new organization is unknown and therefore fearsome. You can overcome this to a degree by introducing organizational change gradually so that participants can grow accustomed to it. You can explain it so thoroughly and so often that the new becomes familiar. You can sell it as an adventure with the promise of excitement and progress.

One aspect here involves gamesmanship—the short-cutting, slightly unethical efforts at self-advancement that are the curse of any change but especially of reorganization. Gamesmanship does go on in a static organization, but all the players know the rules and usually feel reasonably secure. But in reorganization, the rules are new, players are uneasy, the game may go to the clever man rather than to the best man.

To thwart this, explain the new rules, detail the criteria for promotion, and let the players know you will referee objectively and forcefully.

2. The Need for Order

Every reorganization necessitates disorder, at least temporarily. Your remedy: Give a date when the change will be completed, set as early as possible. When a person knows that order, albeit a new order, will return by such and such a date, he can better bear the definitely circumscribed period of turmoil.

Yet make your terminal date realistic or you will land in more trouble than if you had cited no date in the first place. One manager of a reorganization set the completion time three months ahead, failed to meet his own deadline, and so eventually was disappointed in his management of that change.

You can also ease the pain of disorder by setting up an "appeals board" to hear cases of unexpected ramifications arising as a result of the change.

3. Fear of Risk

We'll have more to say in Chapter 16 about how to minimize risk in managing change, but now we can point out that some risk is inevitable in any change. Indeed, you probably cannot make significant innovation without taking some chances. Authorities attest to the importance of risk. Professor Silvan Tomkins of Princeton University believes that "creativity without willingness to gamble is highly improbable."

As a manager of change, remind your people of the rewards of risk-taking. As we have seen, most reorganizations cause upsets at the very least. Nevertheless, successful companies keep changing their structures because the payoffs loom large. Where would General Motors be today if its structure remained the same as when it was founded?

Also, recognize that you can't win them all. If one reorganization won't work, try another, and let your people know that. There's nothing sacred about any form of organization. Sometimes it helps to let everyone know what you will do in the event of failure with the current experiment.

Above all, cut short your losses, and let your people know you will do that, too. The greatest asset a manager of change has is knowing when to stop. This applies particularly to a reorganization that's turning sour. Danger signs include:

- When numerous unexpected problems arise.
- When employee morale remains low.
- When expected benefits of the reorganization don't materialize (but have patience; results may be a year or more in coming).
- When you have trouble staffing the new organization.
- When many good people on the old staff leave.

Another aspect of risk concerns the kinds of chances you choose to take—defensive or offensive. Or, stated another way, you can decide to maximize your gains or minimize your losses. The change manager in the reorganization of the employee relations unit took the offensive. He decided that the defensive exhortations of the past to give more attention to nonunionized employees under the existing setup had not worked sufficiently well. He took the more radical step of splitting the organization to maximize potential gains.

He also explained to his staff precisely what he was doing and why. Because positive action usually proves more appealing to people than negative, the manager of change in this instance used the factor in winning his people's support.

4. The Compulsion to Conform

Managers presiding over reorganization may fail when they succumb to conformity, either in the design of the new structure or in the method of implementing it.

Three types of conformers exist. The first is the consensus conformer, who looks for a solution, needs information, and accepts the opinion of the group as the most likely answer. He rationalizes his conformity as democratic action, never seriously questioning the wisdom of the group's opinion. A medium-sizer maker of housewares fell victim to this error when it reorganized its sales structure to parallel that of its larger competitors.

The fallacy soon surfaced: The larger manufacturers offered a full product line, and their sales organization by classes of products made sense. The smaller outfit had structured its sales effort product by product. In shifting to the class organization, it lost the advantage of individual attention which it had once enjoyed —an advantage which turned out to far offset the expected improvement in sales costs.

A second type, the expedient conformer, believes he has the right answer but goes along with the group on what he thinks is the wrong approach because he "doesn't want to rock the boat." A personnel manager suffered from expedient conformity when he reorganized his union relations function to conform with the structure in other units of the company. "I told them we'd have grief from this," he wailed when his plant went on strike. But he had not told top management loudly enough. After the walkout, he did take a more creative approach: he met with the union and told its leaders that he was returning to some elements of the former structure because of special conditions in the plant.

A third type, the passive conformer, lacks self-confidence and accepts group opinion. He has inadequate self-perception, self-doubt, and anxiety. He feels inferior and tends to panic under stress. A recent college graduate won an assignment to reorganize a company's campus-recruiting effort. He went along with his boss's suggestions on how to do this even though he had doubts about their worth. He thought his reactions merely personal. However, he met with indifferent success in early recruiting ventures and eventually worked up sufficient courage to suggest modifications to his boss. To the youngster's surprise, the manager readily accepted his ideas.

Weigh the pros and cons of conformity in managing organizational change. Sometimes your nonconformist attitude may adversely affect too many people to make it practical. Example: An insurance company wanted to reorganize its method of processing claims, but it abandoned the idea when it considered the paperwork and time involved in explaining the new system to its thousands of policyholders. Example: You wish to streamline the administration of the suggestion plan, but the stand-patters oppose you. The change does not make that much difference to you.

Recognize that conformity is an endemic disease of our time. Always be on guard against it. On the other hand, also recognize that all conformity is not bad. A common organizational design must have something to recommend it, or it would long ago have passed into oblivion. A standard technique for introducing reorganization must have worked at least reasonably well in the past. Examine and consider such designs and practices with an open mind.

Conformity proves so pervasive that we sometimes don't realize we are conforming. One way to attack conformity in your approach to reorganization or any other type of change is to recognize that you suffer from a tendency toward it. If you must answer three or more of the following ten questions negatively, the malady has taken hold in you and should be eliminated:

1. In solving problems, do you ever use any designs or methods you never employed before?

2. Do you ever welcome radical departures from what you have tried before?

3. Will you risk an orginal approach, despite possible adverse effects on yourself or others if it fails?

4. Do you use standard solutions when more original approaches don't appear to measure up after fair trial or consideration?

5. Do you ever sacrifice the simple solution for the more complex one when the latter seems to offer a somewhat better answer to the problem?

6. Honestly, do you enjoy taking calculated risks?

7. Do you ever change minor aspects of your organization just for the sake of a modest shift?

8. Do you often read opinions contrary to your own to learn what "the opposition" is doing and thinking?

9. Do you often express opinions on organization and other matters which represent a minority viewpoint?

10. Do you often question and express skepticism concerning given directives, policies, objectives, values, and ideas?

In managing change creatively, as in other aspects of living, we all need approval. Your ability to recognize symptoms that indicate an excessive need for acceptance constitutes the best means of avoiding the pitfalls of a tendency toward too much conformity.

WHERE TO CONTROL CHANGE

The third general technique for making organizatinal change work for you is to keep control of it. A typical reorganization has a curious faculty of acquiring a direction—even a "life"—of its own. The new sales structure turns out to be about the same as the old. The reorganization in manufacturing doesn't improve quality, as expected. The newly structured accounting department doesn't perform a measurement role, as intended.

Several explanations may account for the loss of control. Sometimes all play a part. The first concerns inadequate planning to control change. We dwelt on this in Chapters 11 and 12. Now we can recapitulate:

1. Make sure the customer or client remains the prime concern in your reorganization. Fulfill his needs. Respond to his desires.

2. Investigate endlessly the need and opportunity for change. Put all change to the test. Narrow the field to the final choice.

3. Make sure that all parties to change agree that it's needed and that they approve it and support it.

4. Make certain that the change is pertinent and relevant.

5. Assure yourself that the timing is right.

6. Determine as well as you can that you can make the change effective.

7. Reassure yourself that you, and not someone else, should manage the change.

Numbers 6 and 7 are crucial and often vexing. Your chance for control diminishes sharply if you have trespassed on someone else's territory. True, the person who should reorganize frequently refuses to do so, so an interloper tries to accomplish this out of a sense of frustration or even desperation. This may be the only solution, but it's a difficult answer because control slips away most easily in incompletely conquered territory.

A second explanation for loss of control lies in the degrees of decisiveness in the decision to change. Winston Churchill said, "Great decisions make great commanders." By this, he meant that when the time for action comes the time of indecision must be thrust aside. Half-heartedness is a common reason for a change's failure. When you have done your planning, act.

A third common explanation for a reorganization gone out of control is the failure to measure its progress. Typically, the manager of organizational change does not provide for any measurements. Less often, his controls prove inadequate. Even though the results of a reorganization are hard to count in higher sales, lower costs, or better profits, you can perform the task subjectively, at least.

For instance, you can set up measurements based on exceptions. If innovation doesn't develop in a pattern that parallels successful and similar shifts, watch out. Also, hark back to your original basis for the change, probably prepared when you sold the idea to your management. What did you forecast as the effect of the change? Its timing? Its benefits? How does reality match the forecast? If it does not match well, what can you do to remedy matters?

A fourth explanation for lack of control stems from people. You may develop a beautiful organization chart, but people in the neat boxes may change the planned organization.

People—how they change and how they change themselves—are such a factor in the total equation of change that we'll devote the next part of this book to them.

part five

People Change

chapter fourteen

The Problem of People

In the midst of the critical times in which he lived, Abraham Lincoln said, "The dogmas of the quiet past are inadequate to the stormy present. The occasion is piled high with difficulty and we must rise to the occasion. As our case is new, so we must think anew and act anew."

Those words still hold true more than a century later—in trying to manage the change going on all around us in technology, methods, organizations, and especially people. Probably the most complex change you will have to deal with is transformations in people themselves.

Alvin Toffler put it this way in *Future Shock:* "To survive, to avert what we have termed future shock, the individual must become infinitely more adaptable and capable than ever before. He must search out totally new ways to anchor himself, for all the old roots—religion, nation, community, family, or profession—are now shaking under the hurricane impact of the accelerative thrust."

As a manager of change, you must help your employees adjust to the "future shock" in their work environment, and you must also make sure that the adjustment is in the best interest of your operation. People are changing in their mores and in their psychology. We'll examine the implications of these mutations on the world of work in the next two chapters. But first, we must speculate on some of the physical characteristics of the future world of work before we can deal with the less tangible—and more difficult—problems of mores and psychology.

THE FUTURE WORLD OF WORK

The U.S. Department of Labor predicts a strong economy throughout the decade of the 1970s, a labor force that will grow by 15 million workers.

Two big "ifs" cloud this fairly pleasant prospect. The forecast is predicated on high employment levels and continuing high productivity. The United States productivity growth rate has fallen in recent years behind those of other countries—far behind those of Japan and the Netherlands.

Positive change among people can help us improve our productivity.

The addition of 15 million to the United States labor force expected during the 1970s—equivalent to adding the total population of the commonwealth of Pennsylvania—will bring the total work force to 100 million by 1980. Young adults aged twenty-five to thirty-four will account for almost half of that growth.

This 50 per cent increase compares with only a 16 per cent gain in the same age group's numbers during the 1960s. During the 1960s, this postwar-baby-boom generation was barely getting a toehold position in the labor force. It's now moving into full maturity. It will not only be a different group of young adults than in the last decade but a different kind of group. We must acknowledge its size and understand its substance.

Secretary of Labor James D. Hodgson gives this view of the new work force: "It will be better educated. It will reflect many of the values of today's young culture. I don't mean the subculture of raffish styles and a predilection for pot, although I expect some of them will have these things, too. What I do mean is less patience, greater expectations, a heightened interest in innovation and creativity, a desire for a voice in decisions. This group will be the first generation having had wide exposure to career counseling, and they have developed some independent concepts about careers. They will not be industrial hippies but industrial 'hopies.' A wise business management will examine their hopes. A competitive edge will flow to those who best meet them."

Why does Secretary Hodgson believe this? Largely because there will be so many of the young adults in the future world of work. An employer will find that on the average one out of four of his employees will be in this age group. For expanding firms, the proportion can easily reach 50 per cent.

They will be in the prime of working life. They will be better educated—almost 80 per cent will have a high school education and one-third will have some college. In the years ahead, this will be the first American generation in the United States work force to whom neither a world war nor a depression has immediate meaning.

Along with this growth increase in young adults, there will be a big decline in growth among those in their teens and early twenties—down from a steep 53 per cent growth rate in the 1960s to only 19 per cent in the 1970s.

This presents an opportunity. For decades we have had an increasingly serious youth unemployment problem—a difficulty that contributed to social unrest. From the 1930s through the 1960s, the problem steadily worsened. In 1930 the youth unemployment rate was about one and a half times the national average. By 1970 it had climbed to five times the average figure.

American society hasn't been able to build a good bridge between the world of school and the world of work. Now, as the size of this group decreases, perhaps we can change that situation.

Another dimension to this problem is the still-rising stream of young blacks entering the work force as teenagers. Their rate of increase during the 1970s will be five times as large as that for whites. During the 1960s, blacks made significant occupational gains. They increased the amount of their formal schooling. They progressed in closing the gap between themselves and their white coworkers. Although they are on the way up, they still have far to go. Their average earnings are still below those of whites, and they still hold more than their share of unskilled jobs. For those blacks with no more than a high-school education, the unemployment rate is about double that for comparable whites

WOMEN AND THE WORLD OF WORK

Women are another group with a problem in the present—and probably future—world of work. The increase in the proportion of working women we experienced throughout the 1960s will continue through the 1970s unabated. Married women in particular, including married women with young children, are streaming into the workplace. Sometimes they aim to help shore up the family incomes; sometimes they simply pursue a new life style.

The majority of employed women would continue their jobs even if they had enough money to live comfortably without working, according to a Labor Department study. Data from the survey, which were obtained from a national sample of 5,000 women aged thirty to forty-four who have been participating in the research project for five years, also show that black women as well as white are interested in keeping jobs even when they don't have to. But a substantial portion of the women demand a better deal in their work.

American men have not been completely fair to their women in this area. They could contribute more than they now do, particularly in the professions and crafts. For example, only about 7 per cent of our physicians are women. In many European countries the percentage more than doubles that—20 per cent in West Germany, for instance. The situation among women lawyers is even worse—only 3 per cent in this country, and the figure hasn't changed in fifteen years. The skilled-craft picture shows even sharper differences. In Sweden, 70 per cent of the overhead crane operators are women. Probably no one has seen a female overhead crane operator in the United States since World War II.

The changing role of women in our economy brings up questions of changing life styles, changing values, and other basic changes. But before we get into that later in this section, let's consider some of the more tangible implications of the rising tide of women in the workforce.

One thing obvious and necessary is day-care centers to permit mothers with young children to work. We must also find new ways to retain women coming back into the labor market. And managers of change must examine part-time job opportunities.

For many people the shorter work week is an increasing reality, made possible partly by a part-time job. And these jobs, increasing at a steady pace, have a lot of advantages for many different kinds of people. For young people, part-time work can be the means to a better education or a means of easing the transition between school and work. For retired people it can mean added income and the opportunity to keep busy. And for women it can eliminate the necessity of a choice between the home and the office.

NEW KINDS OF JOBS

The Labor Department reports that the long-term shift toward white-collar and service occupations will continue. White-collar jobs will be 50 per cent more in evidence than blue-collar positions by 1980. The trend will also continue toward more state and local government workers. Their numbers will increase by more than 50 per cent by the end of this decade. Federal employment, however, may go up only 10 per cent as bureaucracy diminishes on the federal level but increases at the state and local levels.

One sobering thought: These expanding job areas—white-collar, government, and services—traditionally have been areas of poor productivity. Our burgeoning technological, methods, and organizational changes have brought new high levels of productivity to American industry. Can it now do the same to attack sluggish productivity in offices and stores?

PLANNING THE FUTURE

Projections such as the foregoing are useful to throw light on future problems and opportunities—an early-warning system that gives us time to plan for the future, to capitalize on the opportunities that will arise, and to steer around reefs that we can see ahead. We should examine these developments against what we want because we can influence our destinies.

Fundamental to this designing ahead is manpower planning to take advantage of the younger, better-educated work force that will have more blacks and women in it.

Any manager is in the manpower-planning business whether he wants to be or not. He may perform the function well or poorly, depending on how skillfully and seriously he meets his obligations. Performed well, manpower planning offers these advantages:

1. It will give you more flexibility in managing your operation.
2. It will help you obtain and keep better people.
3. It will give your employees a greater sense of accomplishment and stability.

A manager who practices good manpower planning provides for change in his operation by developing "second men" for key positions. Stability and continuity in the organization give you greater opportunity to conceive and take on new projects, improve productivity, and increase quality. Without good manpower planning, you may have to spend much time "fire fighting," trying to solve each manpower problem as it arises.

With good manpower planning, a manager should consistently have better people working for him currently than he did a year earlier. Above all, good manpower planning enables you to keep a high proportion of your people from voluntarily leaving.

When the manpower function is planned, employees themselves are more comfortable. They welcome the sense of purpose and the knowledge that stability is one of the objectives. Stability can be—indeed, must be—achieved in the midst of the changes going on around us. A planned progress and an orderly development in the area of manpower will provide stability even though changes continue.

Four steps prove essential to good manpower planning:

1. Set the target. Get a complete picture of your unit's market forecast to determine the direction the manpower program should take.

2. Take stock. Learn about past productivity rates, employment levels, and turnover rates as well as the present composition of the organization's managerial, technical, and other work forces by experience, age level, and potential.

3. Make a yearly projection. Use the data obtained in step 2 and project your figures one year ahead on the basis of marketing forecasts.

4. Use the projection. The best planning and charts in the world are useless if they are not put to work.

The manager of a large engineering department surveyed his manpower requirements for a decade ahead. He learned that 20 per cent of his engineers would retire over the coming ten years.

In addition, another 15 per cent would probably quit, to judge from past rates. At the time, he employed no blacks or women, so he set out to recruit them on a planned basis. Furthermore, he told black and female candidates about his plans. "The fact that we had a plan laid out for ten years ahead impressed them," he said, "and contributed to our hiring the cream of the crop. When word got out, we found many Negro and women engineers—and there still aren't too many of them—applying for our jobs."

To help insure success of your planning efforts:

1. Get top-management support. The top manager in your component must support the program fully, or it will never get off the charts and forms into action.

2. Get managerial support at all levels. When the general manager approves, the next step is to enlist the wholehearted backing of all the other managerial echelons.

3. Communicate fully and frequently about manpower planning. Don't hide its light under a bushel.

4. Go first class. Give the manpower-planning function status in the organization, and staff the activity with good people. Give it visibility. Manpower planning can determine the future direction of your operation. To do the job right requires the best in people, budgets, and support.

TIME FOR TEACHING

Teaching goes hand in hand with manpower planning as a tool to help design for the future changes among your people. As a manager of innovation, you must teach employees new skills, new attitudes, and new habits that relate to your work.

The best teaching in business emphasizes on-the-job, individual treatment. Oral and on-the-spot visual communication has proved the most practical means of training. Many of the following suggestions may help you in training.

1. Begin with what the employee already knows. This establishes confidence and reduces nervousness. Refer to related experience. Draw parallels. A personnel department changed from conventional typesetting using Linotype and hot-lead techniques to computer setting for its employee publications and manuals. In teaching his publication people about the new techniques, the manager encountered opposition from two older employees who objected to the greater trouble in making changes and in the allegedly inferior appearance of computer-set material. The manager acknowledged the greater difficulty in making changes in layouts, but pointed out that individual line changes were easier than with hot lead provided the shifts occurred before the page makeups were made—just as it is easier to correct rough copy in typescript form than in finished manuscript. He also showed them examples of computer-set material that surpassed hot-lead samples in quality. To clinch his arguments, he took the whole staff on a guided tour through a computer-setting shop.

2. Go ahead bit by bit. Divide the training into manageable segments and do it a step at a time. The manager who shepherded the change in typesetting methods did so, leaving until the end the tour through the computer-setting shop.

3. Repeat. But avoid boredom by repeating in different ways. The personnel manager made his points in several ways, relying heavily on examples of typesetting in actual company publications to convince the recalcitrant people and to teach them how the typesetting method worked, which he realized was more than half the problem.

4. Practice, to make as perfect as possible. The manager used repetition to accomplish this. He also had his people try their hand at typesetting during their tour of the computer shop.

5. Stimulate questions. The manager was careful not to shut off questions from the skeptics because he recognized that seemingly innocuous queries masked their concern. Their antagonism to the new methods soon surfaced in the discussion about the seemingly innocent questions.

6. Try to be positive and encouraging. All people respond best to encouragement. Also, praise in public, but censure in private.

7. Use visual aids when practical. The plant tour in effect was a visual aid to teach the new methods.

8. Show the individual where he belongs in the scene. The manager emphasized the slightly different role the writer must perform when his copy gets set by computer, rather than by the Linotype machine.

9. Show where the work being done fits in. The personnel manager took pains to show that the editor-writer's role remained substantially the same, regardless of how the words got translated into type.

10. Follow through. The manager unobtrusively checked to see how the skeptics, in particular, were making out after the shop tour.

11. Watch for the better "students." The manager also noted that several of his people took to the new techniques with ease. He made a mental note of this for the next change to come.

12. Know when to stop. In a sense, teaching never ends, but certain aspects of it do. When the manager made his point about the ease of correcting copy with the new techniques, he dropped that aspect and went on to something else. You can worry one point so much that you set up counterreactions. Avoid "overkill."

Techniques of instruction, however, often prove less vital than attitude. Ask yourself these questions to test yours:

■ Do I believe in what I teach?

■ Do I regard the "student" as an individual or as a faceless member of a group, such as a black, or a woman, or a "kid"?

■ Am I presenting the material in a way I would like it presented to me?

■ Do I present it clearly and concisely?

■ Have I shown patience?

■ Have I remained calm?

■ Have I shown enthusiasm for the job?

- Have I encouraged the "student" to higher performance?
- Have I corrected mistakes tactfully but unmistakably?
- Have I praised sincerely and generously?
- Have I stimulated questions and comments?
- Have I presented the *why*, in addition to the *what*, of whatever I'm teaching?
- Have I put across the standards of performance expected?
- Have I made clear the rewards for a job well done?
- Have I made clear that employees have the freedom to fail, provided that the failure is because of ignorance or human error rather than willfulness or criminal carelessness?

The question of failure may also apply to your own performance as a teacher. If you don't seem to be getting across, ask yourself questions such as these:

- Have I chosen the right person to teach? Can he take this change, from the standpoint of his skills or his psychology?
- Do I understand fully what I teach? In change, particularly, this proves vital. The personnel manager took a short course in computer typesetting before he tackled his own employees.
- Have I timed my teaching correctly? The personnel manager held off until the skepticism came to light.
- Have I found a reason for teaching? The best teachers instruct so subtly that the learner scarcely realizes it. The personnel manager did this with most of his people.
- Have I appraised the counterinfluences in my teaching? Racial or sexual or generation-gap prejudice—real or imagined—looms here. The problem rarely results because a manager shows blatant prejudice or suffers badly from "foot-in-mouth" disease. The real difficulty in the racial area lies in overcaution—a walking-on-eggs attitude that makes the learner ill at ease. With women or younger people, the teacher may antagonize students through almost unconscious patronizing attitudes, and comments such as "You women perhaps are unaccustomed to . . ." or "When I was your age . . ."

PARENTHESIS ON EDUCATION

Probably the most remarkable phenomenon of the late 1960s and early 1970s—unusual both for its vehemence and for its universality—has been the series of student revolts that hit nations as diverse and dispersed as Japan and France, Italy and Mexico, Pakistan and the United States. Members of your new work force—youth, blacks, and women—may have participated. This phenomenon has generated such emotions that some employers look askance at anyone who has attended college in the last five years.

Yet the odds are strongly against the likelihood that extremism and violence will be continued directly into the world of business.

First, the student radicals probably aren't interested in business. Second, the militant element among students is small (estimates vary from 2 to 5 per cent). Third, many radicals lose their radicalism as the years go on.

However, their mores and psychology undoubtedly differs from that of older people. We'll examine these factors in the next two chapters.

chapter fifteen

Mutations in Mores

Work is a four-letter word.

Are quips of this sort an unhealthy symptom of new American attitudes toward work as a dirty word?

In 1970, the United States experienced more than 35,000 bomb threats and 5,000 actual bombings. Dozens of policemen were shot, not because they were in the act of duty but only because they were symbols of a lawful society.

Do somber statistics such as these indicate a rising tide of American disregard for order and authority?

Of the millions of students currently on our college campuses, each spent an average of 18,000 hours watching television before he or she went to college. This exceeds by 8,000 hours the total time each of these students spent in school while preparing for college. Many TV programs present a problem and solve it completely in thirty or sixty minutes.

Have young people become television-conditioned to think that any problem can be clearly defined and solved within one hour? Are more and more young people demanding instant solutions, resorting even to violence if necessary to bring it about?

THE DECLINE IN AMERICAN PRODUCTIVITY

American managers must learn to live with changing mores in their work force. One result of these changes may have contributed to an alarming decline in productivity in this country. J. J. Jehring, director of the Center for the Study of Productivity Motivation at the University of Wisconsin's Graduate School of Business, has been saying so ever since 1966.

He points to an earlier and parallel trend in England when the country stopped pushing increased production, and stressed redistribution of welfare in its place. "All the motivation was gone," says Jehring. In England, in a single year, incomes rose 8 per cent while production increased 1 per cent, but the English didn't seem to care, he says.

"Today, England is in serious economic trouble. Productivity has fallen, costs have risen, and an unfavorable balance of trade has resulted."

Looking at United States productivity trends leads one to believe an ominous parallel may have begun here, too. Output per manhour (a common measure of productivity) from 1965 through 1970 slowed down to an annual increase of 1.8 per cent in manufacturing, compared with a 3.5 per cent yearly gain in the early 1960s. In 1970, manufacturing posted only a 1.1 per cent increase.

WHAT CAUSES THE SLUMP?

This decline in American productivity comes in the face of great technological gains and dramatic increases in output per manhour in other countries, as the following chart indicates:

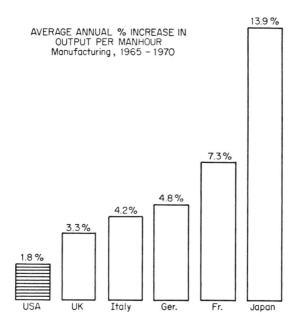

AVERAGE ANNUAL % INCREASE IN
OUTPUT PER MANHOUR
Manufacturing, 1965 – 1970

13.9 %

7.3 %

4.8 %

4.2 %

3.3 %

1.8 %

USA   UK   Italy   Ger.   Fr.   Japan

Why the slump in America? Many factors account for it, but one that may not have been given sufficient weight lies in changing mores. J. Irwin Miller, chairman of Cummins Engine Co., Inc., Columbus, Indiana, expresses the problem this way: "For our predecessors, tomorrow was the clearing and taming of the wilderness, the founding of cities, the building of highways and railroads, the development of universities, the enthusiastic embrace of the Industrial Age. And it was pursued with a vast confidence that we were on the right track and uniquely fitted to succeed.

"Now we are no longer so sure. Where we were once the leaders of change and hope for mankind, now we are fearful of change, and the status quo is our security blanket. . . . When we ask, 'What shall be the national priorities and how shall we allocate the natural resources?' we are asking a question we have never in our history had to ask, a question we never thought we would have to ask."

We are creating a new society, not a changed society. We are simultaneously undergoing a revolution in youth, sex, race, colonial relationships, economics, and technology. Our society is now so diverse, with proliferation going on at such a rate in communication, education, and consumer products, that some people grow paralyzed by the complexity in the diversity of choice.

All the diversity has fostered a stupendous growth in cults, based on occupation, hobby, age, and interests. The engineers give more loyalty to their profession than to their employer. Hobbyists often pursue their interests with a relentless enthusiasm that they seldom give to their job. Many people over fifty tend to resent those not yet forty because of their swift career progress or other "advantages."

Such factors tear society apart at the seams as old alliances and relationships disappear. The old consensuses are cracking. We begin to "consume" life styles ike food—mod, hippie, outdoor, indoor, sport, etc.—because the various life styles offer us a feeling of belonging and a respite from the tensions of change. No wonder that we experience mutations in mores as we experiment with one style after another.

Managers of change must reckon with this phenomenon, recognizing that it will profoundly affect business operations.

Many a foremen today has encountered the hourly employee who refuses to work more than three or four days at a time because he makes enough money in that period to live as comfortably as he pleases for the rest of the week. The move toward the four-day week in a few business and government operations reflects this mutation in mores.

While some employers still resist, most allow clothing and hair styles that would have seemed wildly bizarre only five years ago. The mores have obviously changed here.

A worker in a Detroit axle plant was found not guilty for reasons of temporary insanity of murdering his foreman, another supervisor, and a highly skilled employee. The verdict was widely applauded by his fellow workers because of the "inhuman conditions in this plant." The others' attitude indicates the degree to which some people's mores have turned on questions of justice and retribution. Nor are such feelings confined to blue-collar employees.

MANAGEMENT MUTATIONS

"Executives are stirring. They have been taken for granted. They want to resist the new dronelike atmosphere of their executive workplace." Is this a quotation from a union organizer? A communist? A recent graduate of the Harvard Business School? David Secunda said it. He's vice president of the feet-on-the-ground American Management Association in New York.

Secunda talks about what he calls the "upper third" of employees—between the president and the rank and file. They are the "knowledge workers . . . the vice presidents, the plant managers, the chief engineers, the materials managers." They too, he says, are "part of the now generation. Their fear is that their creation—the well-oiled and smooth-running company machine —now is showing signs of becoming their Frankenstein monster. . . . Those who express a feeling of being victimized or put upon do not single out their bosses or superiors as the culprits as much as they resent the system—the damn company."

Much of this feeling surfaces because younger Americans are moving into management. They want to be heard. They are already moving at a higher velocity than their predecessors, getting promotions faster and responsibility earlier. They press for more of the same. What's more, they come with high hopes acquired at college for improvement of the environment and of society, and they want their companies to work actively toward such goals.

These young managers are something new in the business world. They differ from their predecessors. The young manager of the 1950s, dubbed by *Fortune* as the Organization Man, was reconciled to his role of serving big companies. Although he was determined to preserve his individuality, he was willing to go along with management toward goals the companies judged to be valid.

The young manager of the 1960s, called the Young Executive by *Fortune,* was colder and more pragmatic, zealous and skilled at problem solving, absorbed in his company to the exclusion of almost everything else. *Fortune* judged that "he had no interest in changing corporate life or corporate goals, and he almost never doubted the worth and importance of his role."

By contrast, today's junior managers—2.7 million of them in their twenties, earning $10,000 to $20,000 annually—reflect the passionate concerns of youth in the 1970s for individuality, openness, humanism, concern, and change. If they get no response, their anger at what they see as imperfections in society and business could infect their colleagues and subordinates, resulting in a kind of industrial revolt.

George Koch, president of the Grocery Manufacturers of America, predicted that within five years a group of junior managers will "lock a president of a major corporation out of his office" to force concessions from the company. In this era of accelerated acceleration, such a prediction may become reality in months, not years.

Young managers make two different kinds of demands on their employers. First, they want to work on personal projects they believe socially important—teaching in a street academy, counseling minority small businesses, or carrying out cleanup campaigns and ecology studies. Many believe that such projects merit paid time off from work, but others merely want company sanction.

The second kind of demand lies in the area of corporate policies and objectives. A conference of young management people at Maxwell House, reported by *Fortune* in March 1971, provided a sample of the thinking going on. The General Foods division's top management, drawing up a ten-year management plan and anxious to involve its junior managers, brought a dozen of them together for three days to sound off on what they thought were the shortcomings in division policies.

The company's main shortcoming, as the young critics saw it, was concentrating "unduly" on profits. They did not criticize the concept of profits or their necessity, but did question the way profits are used. They contended that the division should put more of what it took out of the economy in profits back in ways that would improve society.

Although General Foods has made intensive efforts to hire and train blacks, the junior managers concluded that "real results" were few. They also asked that the division make it known that employees were encouraged to involve themselves in social problems. The young managers suggested that a small percentage of the division's advertising budget be allocated for public-service information and that Maxwell House do more research on packaging to find ways to reduce solid-waste pollution. They learned that the division was already doing substantial research on biodegradable materials. At the same time, top management learned that it needed to communicate better what it did in all areas of social-problem research.

Much the same sort of recommendations came from delegates to a White House Conference on Youth. Increased job opportunities for young people and strong stands against pollution were called for. The delegates appealed for recognition of individuals at work as total persons. The thrust of the proposals is that earning a living should be meaningful activity—not drudgery.

Routine jobs, such as assembly-line work, would be improved by "job rotation" and real possibilities of promotion.

Youth called for more participation in an employer's decisions, a company youth advocate to bring management and young employees closer together, and greater efforts by management to explain to each worker his part in the firm's progress.

A proposal to foster executive empathy would have managers "visit all areas of their organization and spend a period of time doing the work of employees" to better appreciate the workers' position. In turn, they suggested, lower-level employees should get a crack at the "responsibilities and perspectives" of the executive level.

AMA's Secunda takes note of proposals such as these as he

questions the ability of modern management to continue functioning in an environment characterized by a stifling atmosphere and less freedom to do what he's supposed to do—manage.

"Isn't it time," he asks, "for an Executive Bill of Rights?" This would be a "set of professionally designed and identified rights worthy of protection and preservation, and adopted by corporations that subscribe to its contents and support the thesis that management is now worthy of being professionalized, necessitating . . . a code of conduct."

Secunda visualizes an Executive Bill of Rights such as these:

- Categories of executive capabilities and commensurate compensation ranges.
- A set of guaranteed relationships between an executive's status and his function.
- Limits on conformity which the corporation would not exceed.
- Social and political freedoms assured.
- Provisions for the development of the executive in management skills.
- Guaranteed severance arrangements.
- Assured rights to any executive of company contributions made to the executive's account for withdrawal or transfer (but never to be lost or forfeited) on an agreed-to basis.

"The time for this alternative," Secunda explains, "to either white-collar unionism or progressive executive atrophy grows shorter even though, to some, it still seems that any such action is not only premature but also irresponsible and reeking of conduct unbecoming to an executive.

"Executive development . . . needs a rebirth with as much emphasis on 'how to be' vice president . . . as it has had to date on 'how to become' one," Secunda says.

"Let's concentrate on our 'upper third' and head off the seeds of possible executive rebellion so that the inevitable growth and power and influence of the jumbo-size corporation will not be as dehumanizing and manipulative as it is charged.

"Furthermore, if we are losing our competitive edge as a nation, perhaps it is because our managers are suffering from inbreeding and are stagnant when it comes to action and stale when it comes to innovation."

He adds: "Who knows? What is good for our managers may be good for our corporations. Give executives their rights as well as their responsibilities and perhaps one day someone might even build a statue to a businessman."

DEALING WITH MUTATIONS IN MORES

If the official of a respected management association and the editors of a prestigious business magazine can speak seriously of changing mores among management men and if the evidence of our eyes and ears tell us of parallel changes among other employees in the world of work, the manager of change must take this phenomenon into account as he deals with the "people" aspects of innovation.

To accomplish this, he first must deal with the "group mind" in which are lodged the mores of the people. The group mind has been a part of man since his prehistoric origins. John Roddam in *The Changing Mind* speculates that man's mind was first a group thing, even though there were individual brains. It was much like herd action. We have mob psychology as the most dramatic remnant of it today. But it persists in "infectious" action with mores on a more subtle level; youths' beliefs and perceptions seep over to their elders. That's one reason why it's important to know how young managers and other youthful employees feel and think.

In the previous section we discussed the organization as an engine to facilitate change. Now we can acknowledge that the organization may inhibit change, largely because it has special trouble in adapting to changing mores. This is because:

■ The organization usually fosters specialization to increase efficiency. The specialized function sometimes cannot deal effectively with generalized mutations in mores.

■ To prevent ambiguity, the command chain in an organization is usually tight rather than flexible. Again, this poses problems when a group's customs and moral attitudes undergo subtle shifts.

■ Rewards in a typical organization are based on the achievement of present goals rather than on innovations directed toward future and more intangible goals. Example: Today, the organization rarely pays a manager an incentive to combat something like pollution, while it will reward him for increasing production which may cause more pollution.

The above doesn't mean that you can't manage change in an organization, but it does suggest that you will have to take special care as you act within the confines of the organization to foment change that may conflict with or challenge new folkways of your employee group. The first precept, then, in dealing with mutations in mores lies in recognizing that your management structure is probably poorly equipped in this area.

Harmonious team spirit may inhibit change if the team "votes" against it. That's why a little disunity helps even—or especially—in the best organization. Not so incidentally, changing group attitudes from within is usually more effective than increasing pressures from without.

A second precept in the area of mores is to expose the new ones throughout management. Familiarity may breed contempt, but it may also reduce the shock among some people over new values and moral attitudes. If the exposure's result remains contempt, you haven't really lost much ground.

A third and related suggestion to cope with mutations in mores is gradually to introduce changes that affect them.

A fourth: Avoid pitfalls that commonly arise with mores. Among many, three stand out. Confusing the cause with the cure frequently occurs. For example, the cause of pollution may be automobiles. But doing away with autos is not necessarily the cure. Confusing appearance with reality takes place often. Because a man wears his hair long today is not evidence that he lacks courage. Confusing practice with a controlled situation is a third hazard. Young managers particularly fall into the trap of believing that a behavioral-science finding will always work out the same way in the real world—for instance, that employees work best as their own bosses. This has proved true, but only in some special situations.

A fifth precept is to use the corporate reward system to stimulate change that involves mores. At least one major company, for example, rewards managers financially whose minority employment reaches a specified level.

A sixth suggestion lies in communication. We'll have more to say on this in Chapter 17. But now we can advise: Communicate vigorously about what you are doing concerning social and other questions that affect mores.

The seventh precept is to act in areas involving mores, despite the difficulties. Too many people want, essentially, to make no decision at all or at best to postpone it as long as possible in a troublesome matter of mores. But this is a decision, too, that may prove the worst of any.

Example: A pharmaceutical firm met with such opposition to a planned expansion that it abandoned ideas of increasing capacity. The opposition arose partly from within its own ranks. Some of its people felt that the expansion would dislodge residents of the area, interfere with the residential-business balance in the community, and lead to undesirable "town and gown" types of hostilities. The predictable happened to the company; when it failed to expand, it began to wither. Eventually it went bankrupt. A different kind of hostility developed when the town residents saw a job market and tax source evaporate through bad management.

Moral: Mores must be taken into account, but within the context of all other business considerations.

An eighth suggestion for coping with mores concerns acceptance rather than reform. As a lone manager or even in concert with a few others, you have faint hope of changing deep-seated social and other beliefs of your employees. If you object to the views of some of your people strongly enough, see that they don't remain your employees, but recognize that you definitely don't have the time and probably don't have the skill or the right to practice group psychology to eliminate mores you believe undesirable. You can go so far as to make clear what you consider proper mores. But most of the time for practical purposes, accept what you find and work with it as best you can.

As we shall see in the next chapter, a parallel situation often arises in the temptation to practice psychology with an individual. We say now, as we will say again: Resist the temptation.

chapter sixteen

Coping with Psychology

When the Burlington Northern railroad was formed by merger in 1970, the Brotherhood of Railway clerks obtained a job-protection agreement. Under this pact, workers in the Chicago regional office were offered transfers to the line's St. Paul, Minnesota, headquarters.

However, a group of forty-one clerical workers refused to go. In their case the agreement specified that the workers nonetheless could not be fired but had to be kept on at full pay, even though there was no work for them to do. In this situation the railroad tried to be understanding and sent some of the nonworking workers home at full pay. But other employees protested, so then the railroad required all forty-one to put in a full, do-nothing day. Dissatisfaction remained among many of the forty-one. "Who wants to sit down all day?" complained one woman in the group. "It's definitely more tiring sitting all day on those hard chairs."

Aside from the irony of the situation, the psychological implications are rife. Reasonable severance pay, relocation, and retraining holds more appeal to most workers than the preservation of useless jobs.

Change nearly always poses psychological threats because it usually upsets mental processes and behavior. The question is not how to avoid such threats in managing change; rarely can that be accomplished. The bypassed threat normally goes underground to surface elsewhere, as in the Burlington Northern case. Rather, the question is how to deal positively with the threat, to render it harmless or, better, to render it useful.

Psychologically passive people generally do not get things done. They have reached their goals, if they had any. They do not consider new ideas on their merits but with reference to established beliefs. They resist innovation. To accomplish change successfully, the manager must stir things up psychologically, but he must do it without pulling things to bits to create nothing but pandemonium.

THE MIND AND CHANGE

Before we suggest what you as a manager can do to avoid pandemonium in your operation when change occurs, let's examine what goes on psychologically when an individual encounters change. Let's look at the human mind. It's not tangible. It's a function, not an entity. It's analogous to the speed of a car. The mind is the function of learning. It's a combination of reason, wile, reflection, intelligence, intellect, perceptual and conceptual thinking, association of ideas, foresight, curiosity, purposefulness, self-control, conscience, sense of humor, creativity, and appreciation.

The physical evolution of man has stood at an approximate standstill for 500,000 years, but not his mind's evolution. We have written story of man—history—for only 7,000 years, 1 per cent of the human story. That 1 per cent indicates the extent of the evolution of the mind. In other words, most of the mind's evolution has taken place in only 1 per cent of man's time on earth. In that period has come most of the change in man's condition, precipitated largely by man's mind.

Prehistoric man was probably an extreme communist—all for one, one for all. No marriage existed, but extreme promiscuity. The group mind prevailed, with little or no self-consciousness. His distinction from lower animals, while early, was blurred. The mind of the individual and the mind of the tribe were virtually indivisible.

The first nonconformists were individualists (whom we now accept as commonplace and admirable) and gave in to self-interest (which we now accept as the criterion by which most men form their judgments).

The first nonconformists were either expelled or became kings, chiefs, or witch doctors. Interestingly, no records exist of tribes who expelled their nonconformists. Those who became leaders changed their tribes, which usually led to greater things.

"The human brain is capable of seemingly unlimited expansion," writes John Roddam, "and . . . if expansion takes place in a direction which offers opportunities of yet further development, then mental evolution is quickened."

As one or a few minds make new discoveries and initiate changes, other quick minds accept the changes, and eventually most minds climb to a new plateau. The invention of movable type for printing was such a change, Einstein's discovery of relativity another, and the development of the computer still another.

All these changes increased the tempo of mental evolution on a breathtaking scale. Most changes may not have such scope, but they can quicken the psychological pace to a degree commensurate with their scale.

Note also that the converse can occur. With no or little

change, a race, a nation, a company, or a person will atrophy. Australian aborigines, Manadarin China, U.S. Electric, and countless individuals have suffered that psychological fate. A deliberate attempt to slow psychological growth may also lead to atrophy—or insurrection. For example, today's revolt of youth may stem from this source. Our conscious lengthening of the educational span has extended adolescence far longer than it was only a century ago. Compounding the problem is the fact that today, because of diet, a boy of 15 is maturer physically (and perhaps mentally) than a 15-year-old of the 1870s, but he must stay in the educational cocoon longer.

From these and earlier observations in this book, we can draw the following conclusions about the individual's psychological reaction to change:

1. The prospect of change upsets most people until they know it doesn't threaten their status or well being.

2. Positive change stimulates most people.

3. A lack of change dulls most people.

4. A lack of change enrages some people, to the extent of revolt.

5. Change tends to have a "Pied Piper" effect; other changes follow good changes, and other people adopt those changes that prove promising.

6. Change that proves it can uplift the spirit wins more converts than change that affects only the flesh.

7. It is more comfortable to prepare for and accept change than to wait until it is forced upon us.

8. Man has the wit to cope with change. Animals have to await, unconsciously, their adaptation to their changing environment in the course of an evolution spread over numberless generations.

9. Man can adapt to change through continuous learning and patience.

10. The history of change shows that when conditions get bet-

ter, people become more openly dissatisfied; they do not give thanks for how far they have advanced, but pray for the distance they want still to go.

11. Change does not necessarily make old values obsolete, although some people think so.

12. The long-term effects of change are invariably more important than the short-term, but few people consider the distant future in embracing change.

THE MANAGER AND PSYCHOLOGICAL ASPECTS OF CHANGE

How can you, as a manager of change, apply these general conclusions to your specific problems as your operation undergoes innovation? You can apply them by paying careful, balanced attention to requirements that behavioral research indicates typical employees want a job package to fulfill in these nine basic areas:

1. Good pay and other material benefits
2. Good working conditions
3. Good bosses
4. A fair chance to get ahead
5. Steady work
6. Respectful treatment
7. Rewarding association on the job
8. Important and significant work
9. Full information

Woe to the manager of change who attempts to initiate an innovation that poses a threat to any of those. Woe to the manager of change who gives unbalanced attention to the nine so that one area gets undue consideration. In the railroad case, management and union leaders concentrated on steady work and pay to the detriment of important and significant work and several other of the nine basic areas. As a result of the imbalance, they found themselves facing psychological problems.

Coping with psychological problems caused or aggravated by change does not mean that you as a manager try to practice psychology. As we pointed out in the last chapter, you definitely don't have the time and probably don't possess the qualifications to do so. Rather, you will deal most successfully with psychological difficulties by using more practical and mundane remedies. If you can give balanced and careful attention to each of the nine job-package areas, you will go far toward meeting the psychological implications of the changes you seek to introduce. Let's examine each of the nine areas in detail to try to determine what constitutes appropriate action:

1. *Good pay and other material benefits.* Each employee should be paid in accordance with his job requirements to a level that is, generally, equal to or better than the average that others in his community receive for similar work.

An increasingly important part of each employee's compensation lies outside his take-home pay. Benefit programs should be imaginatively competitive with those of other employers. These programs should recognize the differing needs of individuals. They should enable each employee to protect himself and his family against serious financial loss from such hazards as illness, disability, and death; help provide for an income after retirement; and enhance the general well-being of employees by providing time for personal business and leisure through vacations, holidays, and other arrangements. In combination with public programs and prudent private arrangements, these programs should make financial security both before and after retirement an attainable goal.

If the compensation package is right, a man will think twice about quitting because of a change and may temper his protest at innovation.

2. *Good working conditions.* You should provide work areas that are safe and attractive. Work schedules should be planned

so that each employee can enjoy his leisure time in balanced measure with his work time. Most people do not live to work, but rather work to live.

3. *Good bosses.* In addition to technical competence, the criteria for selecting an employee to supervise the work of others should include his ability to deal fairly and successfully with his subordinates. Where necessary, training should be provided to insure that these characteristics are developed.

Further, you should recognize that no supervisor or system is perfect. Therefore, a formal procedure should be established for employees to carry problems and complaints to higher levels for consideration and adjustment.

4. *A fair chance to get ahead.* The best personnel development takes place on the job. Make it clear that you believe and practice this. While courses outside the organization may help, the key to teaching new skills or relationships that may be necessitated by change lies on the job itself.

A manager in New England failed to get his change accepted because he failed to provide adequate on-the-job training in the new machine he had persuaded the management to buy. He relied too heavily on training at the equipment builder's plant.

Everyone has the right to expect a regular review of his performance from his supervisor. The most important aspect of such a review is a full, two-way discussion of how well each individual is performing in his present assignment and how well he is living up to standards of excellence and performance that should be clearly defined.

Your communicated policy should be that you hire qualified employees, aid them in self-development, and advance them to positions of higher pay and responsibility as openings occur. Although no enterprise can thrive on an ironclad policy of promotion solely from within and of advancement by strict seniority, you should make it your general practice to promote from within and to promote the more senior employee, all other qualifications being equal.

5. Steady work. Each individual employee should have the assurance that his day-in, day-out performance builds security for him and his family. While absolute job security is not possible, make known your intention that an individual who performs long and competently will have greater security in his job than an individual whose tenure is shorter and competence less.

6. Respectful treatment. You must recognize individual worth and human dignity of each employee. This requires a system of management and an organization that can insure that each business decision is made only after the impact on people is carefully weighed and has itself become a factor in the decision.

No individual can be forced to do his best; the growth and prosperity of your operation depends on the willingness of each individual to do his job well. This voluntary best effort builds operations and assures a vital future.

7. Rewarding association on the job. Create an atmosphere for maximum team effort. How can you do this? By focusing on the wants and needs of the customers or people you serve and by figuring how all of you can best marshal your resources to that end.

Rewarding associations on the job also derive from balanced attention to the previous six job requirements and the next two.

8. Important and significant work. Another job requirement is that it be important and significant. The task must serve some socially useful purposes by providing goods and services that are needed and desired. You can best achieve this aim if each employee understands how he contributes to socially desirable ends.

In his *Apology*, Socrates shows that he wanted reform and change, but he appealed to reason, fair play, justice, conscience, and man's dream of a better self and a better world. Idealism, sincerely held, aids handsomely in coping with psychology because it appeals to the spirit. The spirit can do more than the flesh in fostering change.

The manager of a lamp plant never said, "We make light

bulbs," but "We make light for people to see by." With this and other uncommon turns to commonplace business language, he imparted an idealistic tone to his operations. It was no accident that he eventually changed his plant's productivity from the lowest to the highest in the industry.

9. Full Information. To achieve the foregoing eight job needs, you must communicate. So important is this requirement that we will devote the next chapter to it. But now we can point out that each individual wants and needs to know and understand the goals and propsects of his operation so that he can make intelligent contributions and decisions. In addition, everyone has insights, suggestions, and preferences that can and do affect the course and success of innovation.

In the area of change, each employee should feel free to discuss such matters with his immediate manager, the personnel manager, and/or his manager's manager. But the immediate manager should make it clear that such discussions ought to come with him first.

It is not sufficient simply to express good intentions at the top. Good communication on change should aim at the following objectives:

- The development of a clear statement of intentions relative to a change.

- General awareness and understanding of those intentions by employees, particularly those with managerial responsibility.

- Adequate training and support to employees with managerial responsibilities to enable them to act in accordance with the intentions.

- Provision for building in the decision-making process requirements for consideration of human resources.

- Regular measurements of management performance, including provision for communication and evaluation from employees.

- Provision for promptly admitting and correcting mistakes that are made.

THE ELEMENT OF RISK

Balanced attention to the nine elements that employees want in their jobs will help you cope with *their* psychological problems caused or aggravated by change, but what about *your* psychological difficulties? The nine-element job package will help you, too, but you have a special challenge as a manager of change. It's risk.

All change carries a degree of risk with it. Taking personal risks—which means moving beyond the expectations of your peers and your boss—can prove successful if your risk taking is securely grounded in your power and authority. But these two factors aren't the same. When you seek to reap the benefits of change, you should understand the different ways power and authority operate.

Authority is the authorization you need to perform certain acts, make decisions, or commit the organization's future. You derive authority from the organization through formally delegated authority, from peers who agree on the extent of your authority, and from yourself when you assume responsibility.

The more you move from delegated authority to self-derived responsibility, the more risk you must take. When you claim no authority to perform an independent act of judgment, you disclaim personal responsibility in order to avoid risk. When you look to see what your peers are doing instead, you seek safety from their support. But when you act, even though knowing that "it may be my neck," you take a chance on your own authority.

Taking such a risk could be disastrous if you have no power. Power—the ability to control the behavior of others—directly affects the way you can implement change. Without power, any kind of authority is worthless; with power, any kind of authority has less risk attached. As a manager of change, examine the sources of your power, sources more varied than those of authority.

The first source is friendship. The network of social relations within the organization, both horizontally and vertically, can give you a prime source of power. Is your boss also your friend, especially in a time of upsetting change? Will your peers be sufficient friends to support you?

This friendship doesn't necessarily have to find expression in off-the-job socializing, but that helps.

The second source lies in desirable personal traits. Self-confidence outshines all others, including the degree you can communicate it to others. Paradoxically, this does not mean you must assume an aura of infallibility. Admitting your mistakes may prove the best way in which you can persuade your people to trust your judgment.

Other desirable traits include coolness under fire, honesty, and objectivity.

Opportunity is the third source for power. Can you get your boss' attention quickly? Do you have quick access to your peers?

Another key power source lies in your expertise and information. How good are they? How do others regard them? A quiet, unassuming man became the most powerful figure in a personnel department because he knew the facts and had the expertise about wage rates. To him went the task of implementing a change from incentive to day-work pay in a mideastern company's four plants. To him eventually went the vice-presidency for personnel.

Status helps as a source for power, but probably not as much as in the past. The plush office and reserved parking place have dimmed as symbols. True status derives from less superficial indications, seldom discussed but closely observed. The sales manager who survived three marketing department reorganizations has demonstrated he possesses something the company values, and that gives him status.

Seniority influences a man's power, although this source had declined sharply in recent years.

Proprietorship helps, too, especially in smaller organizations. If you are a substantial stockholder, this carries clout.

Finally, interpersonal skills—communication—will impact greatly on your power base. We'll reserve more discussion about that to the next chapter.

The key to becoming a successful implementer of innovation lies in accurately assessing your power base and taking a little more authority than your base theoretically allows. But in the meantime, you would be wise to bone up on the skills that will increase your power base—to minimize the risk as you manage change.

chapter seventeen

Communicating Change

In the late 1940s, the management in a Southern textile mill decided to merge two small and similar sections in a new location,
with new equipment and better working conditions. At that
time, some of the benefits of good communication were not as
apparent as today, so management determined to try an experiment. Employees in one operation to be moved were told nothing about the impending action. Employees in the other were
kept fully informed about why the change was necessary, when it
would occur, how it would be accomplished, how it would affect
everyone concerned, and the benefits expected from it.

When the moving day was finally announced to the uninformed group, they almost went on strike. But the informed employees took the change in stride, shifting to their new work stations with a minimum of lost production, no grievances, and

high morale. The informed group was happy because the members saw that the promises of benefits had been carried out. The same benefits were available to the uninformed group, but they were too upset by the surprise to note them.

The case illustrates an old truth: It is not enough just to be good; you have to make it well known that you are good. As a corollary to this, you must merit the reputation you communicate and make good on your promises concerning a change. Through good communication, you can help people accept, even sometimes welcome change.

That can be glibly said, but how do you managers do it? By careful attention to these six basic communication prescriptions:

1. Get in on the ground floor of change.
2. Report all the facts of change quickly and completely.
3. Observe the fundamental common denominators of communication.
4. Generate good communication practices in others, especially other managers and supervisors.
5. Use all forms of communication—informal and formal.
6. Be ready for emergencies.

Let's look in more detail at each of the six basics:

1. Get in on the ground floor

A manager should, as a matter of course, be present or informed at the onset of the planning for change, no matter where the change may originate. Of course, if you originate the change, this is no problem. But in many changes, you don't get in at the start. Indeed, you may not get in until near the end when the change is about to be implemented.

You should be involved in the very decision itself because the question of how to communicate a change should be considered from the outset.

"But nobody told me about that," is one of the most revealing excuses a manager can make. It reveals either that he has not been alert enough to inform himself about plans or that the originators of the change did not consider him important enough to inform.

True, sometimes other managers deliberately will not cooperate. Patient education is the only way to correct such situations. Yet most people basically want to cooperate. Your first communication is with the managers that initiate most changes (if you don't) to let them know your interest, why you have it, and how you can help them put the change across smoothly and quickly.

Failure to get in at the outset has been called the Ellis Island approach. The manager then is like the immigrant who comes in long after the mainstream of history has started. Some immigrants have done well, but they start with a serious handicap. So is the manager handicapped who comes onto the scene after the flow of the change has already begun.

2. Report all the facts of change

This appears obvious, but many communication failures start here. The following checklist may help to cover the bases in announcing a change:

■ What's the reason for the change—technological developments, customer requirements, competitive conditions, business conditions? Include goals for new arrangements.

■ Why is the course being followed the best under the existing circumstances?

■ What are the details of the plan?

■ How will employees be affected? Benefited?

■ What is management doing to minimize the impact or the adverse effects of the change on employees? Has full management support been pledged to solve foreseen and unforeseen problems?

■ Have unavoidable work dislocations, delays, or problems been explained in advance?

■ Has employees' support been enlisted to help minimize any problems?

■ Have you reported progress in making the change and overcoming the problems encountered during the entire period of the change?

■ Have you expressed appreciation for the efforts of employees in making the change and achieving the results expected?

3. Observe communication's common denominators

Besides giving the facts of change, you have to do it with correct techniques to get maximum results. For some of the common denominators of any kind of good communication, see page 155 in Chapter 13. Besides explaining reasons for change, naming benefits, inviting participation, avoiding surprise, acknowledging rough spots, setting standards, contacting informal leaders, praising, and repeating, here are other basics:

■ Communicate more or less continuously. In a change situation, you have to communicate before, during, and after the change to get good results.

■ Deal with both big and little matters with equal care and thoroughness. Your little changes are your "samples," evidence that you can perform well when big changes come along. An inadequate performance on a small affair may jeopardize your credibility when a big one comes along.

■ Be concrete and specific. Good communication shows as much as it tells. Vague communication is always bad, but it's especially undesirable in a situation of change because people affected are undoubtedly uneasy and anxious to learn details. Imprecise communication may be worse than no communication at all. More than one change has failed because of this shortcoming in communication.

■ Acknowledge risk and report steps planned to minimize it.

■ Acknowledge difficulties, but put them in proper perspective. Opinion Research Corporation studies indicate that employees want both the good news and the bad about the forthcoming change. When they don't hear about problems, they grow suspicious. But don't exaggerate the problems either. Watch out for the human tendency to dramatize. Be realistic and honest.

■ Know your audience. This seems obvious, but many people overlook the obvious. For instance, some managers remain oblivious to what motivates people generally or their own people individually. Consequently, they don't communicate in terms of their employees' motivational interests, and the bulk of their message is lost. We'll have more to say about this in the next chapter. A knowledge of your people involves understanding on another level. Your audience has prejudices, limits of knowledge, and understanding. Judge the boundaries accurately and communicate in the range of what your people already know and accept. For example, in announcing a new equipment installation, think twice before you ascribe it to the necessity for meeting foreign competition. Most hourly people know there's such competition, but it's still remote to them. Instead, ascribe the installation to the need to cut costs, a necessity with which they are familiar.

■ Know your purpose. Keep it always in mind. A manager of about forty women engaged in repetitive manufacture had trouble with one who couldn't keep up with new performance standards changed by time and motion study specialists. The manager could have discharged her, but his purpose was to keep employees, not fire them. He had another, top-performing employee coach her, and the results proved miraculous.

■ Think and organize. Better to say nothing than to say something unwise. Also, better to say nothing than to be so wordy and disjointed that your people can't understand you or, worse, will misunderstand you.

■ Guard your credibility. It's difficult to acquire, easy to lose, and your most valuable asset. A common test of credibility comes in the small things. Do you give deadlines that are actually shorter than necessary? Do you make "mountains of molehills" by exaggerating the impact of minor changes? Such subterfuges fool almost no one for long. All they accomplish is to damage your own credibility, and that could be fatal.

■ Act on what you say. Inaction or slow action on what you promise often is the most common difficulty. Make no commitments unless you have reasonable certainty that you can act upon them. If you promise to do something and then find that you cannot, report the fact promptly. Tell why you can't perform as anticipated; tell what you plan to do under the altered circumstances. Take prompt action because action delayed can turn out to be almost as bad as none at all. Of course, let your people know you have acted.

■ Communicate in small doses. In complex changes particularly, give the information in manageable portions. But make your bit-by-bit approach consistent and persistent. Tell the same, continued story when you divide your story into smaller parts.

4. Use all forms of communication

Communication failures result because some forms of communication are neglected. Most communication takes the form of informal oral or written varieties. Use them all, but especially oral.

One good use of the informal oral approach occurred at a General Electric location where the union rattled its sabers when plant management lowered several job rates.

Using some of the suggestions we have been talking about, managers and foremen quickly spread the word among many employees, not just those immediately affected. The net result of this informal oral approach was that the union quieted down and withdrew a grievance.

The formal oral approach should not be overlooked either. Many plants have used a round-table approach.

Weekly meetings of about twenty participants run almost continually. A plant manager or one of his staff is often the leader. Participants are a cross section of total employment at each meeting, including supervisors. They get invited on a rotating basis one week in advance. They can submit questions in advance.

The leader has a three- or four-item agenda on such matters as employment, the business situation, or similar subjects. Fears have proved groundless that these sessions would degenerate into griping meetings.

The greatest opportunity lies in the oral areas. We need more and better use of the spoken word by all managers to "sell" the need for and value of change.

Another form of communication that you should be aware of in dealing with change is the nonverbal. You talk with more than your voice. Your eyes, your facial expressions, your gestures all say almost as much as your words.

Don't spoil the good effect of your spoken words with frowns and grimaces that belie your speech. An actor's device may help you. Practice in front of a mirror or before your wife. You may not realize that you habitually frown when you give an order or that you tend not to look your listener in the eye when you talk to him.

5. Generate good communication practices in other managers

Communication will never prove fully effective if only the top manager tries to do the job. All management people must perform the task.

Studies show that a good manager spends as much as 90 per cent of his time communicating. In fact, his job *is* communicating. He spends usually 10 per cent of his communicating time in writing, 15 per cent in reading, 30 per cent in speaking, and 45 per cent in listening. All people who accomplish work through supervising others do the job mostly by listening and talking. We should spend more time on the change aspects of our work.

6. Be ready for emergencies

Usually when you communicate about major change, you have plenty of time in which to do it. But what happens when something occurs unexpectedly and there's not time for a warning well ahead of the event?

If you're in good shape on the first five basics, you won't get caught when emergencies arise.

In emergencies especially, some of your people are not likely to have it in them to respond positively. You will also miss the mark occasionally through your own errors. Learn from the mistake and do better next time. But act positively in your own failures. Shake them off and go on.

Reuel L. Howe, founder and director of the Institute for Advanced Pastoral Studies, in his book *The Miracle of Dialogue* observes that, "Communication means life or death to persons." He continues in a philosophical context which also holds for communication in business: "To say that communication is a problem is to say nothing new, for men always have had to strive to make themselves understood. Each age, however, has its own peculiar communication problems; and our age, possessing as it does an amazing means for increasing, extending, and amplifying communication, confronts in the process both greater potentials and greater frustrations."

FEEDBACK AND CHANGE

If change is constant, resistance to change need not be constant, too. The acceptance of change is partly a problem in communication, for suspicion is a child of ignorance. If employees—managers, professionals, and hourly workers alike—were told what is coming, when it is coming, and how it will affect them, half of the resentment and anxiety could be eliminated.

The opposition to innovation is seldom rational. The negative reaction is not so much resistance to progress as to unscheduled actions which challenge ego or status.

The answer to phobias about change is candor. Honesty and consideration will pave the way for changes that are essential in today's changing world.

A step in that direction is an adequate communication program.

Such a program is two-way. Thus far, we have discussed mostly one side of the communication equation—how you should communicate with the people involved in the change you seek to implement. But they should communicate with you, too, to provide feedback.

Dr. Earle B. Barnes, a Dow Chemical Company vice president, says, "Before a top manager can make intelligent decisions, particularly those required to instigate needed change, he must have ready access to something else which is not always so easily acquired. Before he can prescribe for what is wrong, he must know what the majority of competent people think is right."

Europeans have been analyzing their corporate management skill as compared with that of the United States. *The Economist* noted that American businessmen "are practitioners of the management structure known for no good reason as 'high downstream coupling'—signifying that all the department heads of a company—research, sales, production, finance—work as a group, as opposed to the system of rigidly separated responsibilities in which horizontal communication between various functions is often reduced and which cannot respond quickly to a fast changing environment."

That describes an organization with good feedback—a device that permits rapid flow of information back and forth through the management network, reaching out with sensitive antennae for the first signal of change and allowing maximum time for the organization to get conditioned.

You need to know from your people answers to questions such as these: Are the right signals being given? Are they participating in the changes? Are the changes too fast? Too slow? Are we overcommitting resources? Undercommitting? Are we forcing too much change? Too little?

You need feedback to anticipate both internal and external changes, so that decisions can be revised and so that everyone concerned can be alerted to the necessity of reprogramming activities.

Feedback is also the mechanism for established confidence and credibility. When feedback works, interest and confidence are established.

Feedback is a method of measuring or keeping score on your communication effectiveness. The best gauge is the overall job your people do in handling the change. If they do poorly, look to your communication for at least part of the guilt. If they do well, still check regularly on how you're getting across. You can always do better.

Many other indications hint at communication askew. These include high absenteeism, substantial turnover, scarce suggestions, many grievances, a number of disciplinary suspensions, etc.

But many of these signals come after the fact. You need faster signs of trouble, or success. One approach: Win such high confidence and respect from your people that they will tell you promptly if you are or are not coming through. But they won't feed back to you automatically. Let them know you want their reactions. Prove that you sincerely want the results, even when unfavorable.

And when you have an effective feedback system, pay attention to it. Listen.

Listening is an important part of communicating. You can't do it if you can't stop talking. Listen quietly, attentively, courteously. A good communicator spends more time listening than talking. What's your ratio?

If objective evaluation shows that you talk more than you listen, try some of these devices: Don't interrupt. Pause before you answer questions or respond to comments. The other may not be finished—just catching his breath or collecting his thoughts. Ask for comments and opinions. Show interest; hide boredom or impatience.

chapter eighteen

Motivating for Change

Most good managers see themselves as decision makers. They decide what needs to be done, how much to do, when to do it, how it should be done, and who should do it. They get their cues from a variety of sources, define the mission, then parcel out pieces as individual tasks. In the tradition of the giants of management thinking, Taylor, Gilbreth, and Gantt, they look for the "one best way" for each task, see that employees get trained in the latest techniques, develop rewards and penalties to support their goals and schedules, then "carrot-and-stick" everybody until things get done.

This works now and has worked for years. The manager doesn't try to run the show. He doesn't do the job himself. He plans and organizes individual tasks that contribute to the main goal. He measures and rewards good performance in support of that goal. Undoubtedly, a good manager operating this way gets things done. He's a decider, a controller, a supervisor, a director, but is he a manager, especially of change?

How much does this kind of manager add to the process, particularly compared to what he might add if he took a different view of his job?

There is another way—and one better suited to the management of change. Hugh Estes, a consultant for organization planning at General Electric, says, "Suppose the manager sees himself primarily as the multiplier of the work of others. His primary task then is to make it possible to do more in concert than separately. Whatever the tasks he does himself, whatever plans or decisions he makes, and whatever he sets his mind to, he acts in the context of how it will help those in his organization do a better, faster, and more effective job. . . . He has to assume—and believe it so deeply that it becomes part of his whole approach to his job—that most people most of the time want to learn, want to grow, want to contribute the unique knowledge and information that each knows he has, and want a share in the success of a common effort."

That's another way of saying that the multiplier manager is a motivating manager. He's future-oriented. He constantly makes appraisals, tries to get a better idea on how well those who report to him invest in the future—both in their own and the future of the business. The motivating or multiplying manager develops a questioning attitude of mind that always aims at the future. He asks questions such as these:

■ When was that machine tool last overhauled? (A sloppy maintenance schedule may mean a deteriorating plant.)

■ When were professional employees last considered for raises? (If delay has occurred here, morale sags and employees with much future potential may leave.)

■ How do our products compare with those of competitors? (Slippage here augurs ill for the future.)

■ How do we rate in the community? (A militant union, oner-
ous taxes, even riots in this day and age could result sometime in
the future if the community turns against you.)

■ How did our last advertising campaign fare? (Sound advertising invests in future sales; bad advertising steals from the present.)

■ Should we open a new market in the south now? What
should we spend if we decide to do so? (This must be decided on
the basis of information you gather now. You must become skill-
ful in finding it.)

THE LITTLE BAND OF INNOVATORS

When it comes to change, there's a little band of innovators, a
great group of conservatives, and a little band of inhibitors.

Inhibitors usually develop when they see a threat to their status. Examples:

■ A couple of industrial engineers had a product idea and received the green light. But they were blocked on facilities and
other necessities by the manager of the product-development department who saw (probably correctly) a threat to his operation.
When he finagled a transfer of the project to his department, all
went well.

■ Earlier in this century safety shoes were introduced. They
did not go over well at first because the heavy, clumsy footwear
signaled the wearer as a lower-status factory worker. When the
shoes were redesigned to conform to a dress shoe's appearance,
they went over well.

The overwhelming majority of people are conservatives—
neither for nor against change as such. They accept on faith the
"wisdom of their predecessors"—all overhead is bad, the existing
organization is sacrosanct, etc. "Show me" is their badge. We
need conservatives. We would have no cohesion and continuity

without them because they provide stability. When they can be convinced, they will buy the new idea.

You as the innovator must convince them. You may find yourself as an innovator apparently half-accidentally, but a pattern exists that often develops like this:

1. At the outset officialdom usually resists the new idea.
2. Promoters emerge in response to resistance. Often, the promoter is different than the inventor.
3. Promoters usually promote through informal channels.
4. Typically, one man emerges as the idea's champion. If not, the idea dies.

MULTIPLIER MANAGER AS MOTIVATOR

The multiplier manager, to be a successful motivator, must persuade. Let's look at what's involved:

First, you have to state your conclusions—make crystal-clear where you stand and why. Yet don't let facts alone speak for themselves. Your listeners perhaps won't draw the same conclusions from the facts that you do. But your conclusions must have logic and must respond to a perceived need. In formulating your conclusions, ask yourself questions such as these to prepare a correct strategy of the situation. How can your conclusions be expressed in the most palatable form? How will the conclusions look to the listeners? What's the true nature of the problem?

The second principle stems from the first. Emotions persuade more effectively than facts, especially in the short run. Of course you must have facts, but you need to garnish them with emotion. When putting across change, you must make clear that you believe in the change. You must demonstrate that you intend to pursue the innovation with every ounce of energy at your command. As we have said in several other connections, halfheartedness proves one of the most pronounced dampeners to change that's known. If you don't believe completely in the change, don't pursue it.

The third principle of motivation is: Take your time. Don't try to rush people into acceptance because that will probably just put their backs up.

Another basic falls in the area of resistance. We have mentioned before that you should always expect it in changing times.

Now we can add that resistance is natural and far more common than agreement. Many an employee seems to accept change, but then he continues exactly as he has in the past. Your worst mistake would be to grow angry at resistance. You would be wiser to grow suspicious at too-quick acceptance.

A fifth principle involves personal involvement. You can best achieve it by showing your people that it's in their enlightened self-interest to do things in a new way. Managers in a machine-tool manufacturing plant "sold" a new job classification plan to crane operators and their helpers by showing that the new system gave equal or higher pay to the men and that the helpers who would lose their crane jobs would win new positions at the same or better pay in other parts of the plant.

A sixth basic: Show that the desired action is possible. When you meet the inevitable resistance, overcome it with personal involvement. And you can't get that until you show the feasibility of what you want done. In the machine-tool plant, the managers showed that new jobs were waiting for the displaced men.

Finally, state your motives. We often lose our way here. For some reason, many people think self-interest is somehow dishonorable. We explain a new job-classification system as necessary because "fluctuations in demand no longer make the old system workable." We find euphemisms for new safety standards. Some of the euphemisms may hold some validity, but the real explanation may be a desire for greater efficiency and improved profits. Why not say so? What's wrong with efficiency and profits? They sustain jobs by keeping the business healthy. There's nothing dishonorable about either. When you try to cover up your true or more important motives, you make them seem dishonorable. Use self-interest frankly as part of your argument. If you have the self-interest, the people whom you wish to motivate probably will have it too, so your admission of it can serve as a persuasive argument.

THE CLIMATE FOR MOTIVATION

Yet the foregoing basics for persuasion will prove almost useless if the motivational climate is arid. You must start far in advance to prepare that climate. These actions may help you in that task:

1. *Make the facts of works and work relationships serve you.* Mutual respect that you build between yourself and your employees is essential in motivation. You also need a good climate of respect among your people for each other. If that doesn't exist, you will encounter infinite trouble in persuading employees individually because other tensions and negative factors will offset your efforts. Motivation is usually a team proposition. Stimulate one man, and he'll help you convince the next. But if the first employee doesn't like or trust the second, the conversion of the first won't help with the second.

Make sure that you have the right feelings about your job, too. If you feel cynicism, listlessness, or doubt about the value or importance of your work, it will probably show through and infect your employees. Motivation is an emotional process. Cynicism and the other maladies deaden the emotions, sometimes so seriously that motivation becomes almost impossible.

2. *Let your people know how you feel about the job.* The negative emotions have a way, unfortunately, of showing through despite your efforts to conceal them. Yet, some managers feel uneasy at displaying positive feelings—reticent about expressing enthusiasm concerning the dignity of work, the values of friendship, or the worth of what you do.

American folklore which honors the "strong, silent type" may explain some of this inhibition. The problem becomes more seri-

ous with men than women, which could be one reason why females often make good managers. Such inhibitions prove serious
because your people may interpret your reticence as indifference,
displeasure, or even cynicism.

3. *Talk up, not down, to your employees.* Condescension is
fatal, particularly in these times of human-liberation movements.
Talking down deadens initiative.

A company established a new plant in the south and provided
a cadre of managers and supervisors from its old facilities to start
the new operation. One supervisor in the cadre made it clear to
the raw recruits off the farms that he held a dim view of their in-
experience and amateurism. When the plant manager discovered
this gaffe, he told the supervisor to mend his ways, and he called
all the supervisor's people to a meeting where he said something like this:

"I salute you who are doing an unfamiliar job to the best of
your ability. When you have learned to do it well—which you
soon will be able to do, or we are performing poorly in teaching
it to you—you will be true professionals. You were not born in
an area where your fathers or older brothers did such work before you, to give you an idea of what was ahead even before you
entered this building. That may be a slight handicap. But the
circumstances hold more pluses than minuses. You start with a
clean slate, without misconceptions about this job. Many of you
will soon learn that you have many natural abilities for this
work. We look forward to helping you discover them."

4. *Watch out for dictatorial and paternal attitudes.* In
such a climate you motivate on the superficial level only. In today's human-liberation climate, particularly, these attitudes won't
do. Paternalism probably poses a more serious danger than
naked dictatorship. You can't really motivate under the purchase
plan, which is what paternalism actually is. You try to buy loyalty with promises of protection or favors.

In a reorganization, the manager promised to "take care of"
two favorites. In a way, he did. The organizational change failed,

and the manager and the two cronies ended out on the street.

5. *Accept others' viewpoints where possible.* Nobody knows all the answers, including you. If you won't or don't listen, you may miss the crucial suggestion that will make the change successful. Rarely does an innovation spring full-grown from somebody's head. It develops and grows gradually from several or even many other influences.

6. *Make your changes in a timely way.* Leonardo Da Vinci conceived of manned flight centuries before it actually became possible. The electric car failed in the 1920s, but it may return in the 1970s. History is replete with good ideas that came at bad times. Intuition plays a large part in determining the timeliness of your change. But to help your instincts, ask yourself questions such as these: Is the idea for the change fully developed? Are my employees prepared for it? Can I act on it now, even if they do accept it? Will the change, if adopted, conflict with any projects already under way? If the answer to all these questions is yes, your proposal for change will probably prove timely.

When you have acted upon the foregoing climate-building suggestions and the others previously mentioned, you are ready to motivate your employees for change. Then the basics of communication mentioned in the last chapter will prove their usefulness. In addition, here are a few others that apply particularly to motivation:

First, lead your people gradually to the change. Don't spring the proposal on anybody without preamble. One technique is to ask questions, which could go like this to win support for an equipment change, for instance: Is the old machine holding up? How much downtime did you have on it last month? How's the quality? Can you still make your incentive rates on it? Have you seen the new models? What do you think of them? I need your support for a new machine if I propose it to the boss. Do I have it?

Second, don't make the issue any bigger than it really is. If you want to install new equipment, don't make the move sound like

some vast automation project. If you wish to change job classifications, carefully define what classes you propose to change.
Communicate your proposals to your entire unit, not just those
immediately affected. You should do this to counteract as much
as possible the side effects that almost invariably develop in a
change. Rumors thrive especially when there's little or no information. People not communicated with directly—and probably
not immediately affected—will allow their imaginations to roam.
The people involved may take seriously some erroneous rumor if
it comes from someone within the unit not favored with the
proper communication. Then your motivational efforts suffer.

Third, backtrack when necessary. If you don't get across, try
again, but in a different way if possible.

Fourth, stay cool. Never show exasperation when you don't get
across the first, or even the second or third, time. When you fail
to motivate your people, ask yourself if your strategy was right,
your position correct.

MOTIVATING YOUNG
PEOPLE TO CHANGE

Consider the foregoing principles and suggestions in the light of
motivating young people in change situations. It will help to do
this for three reasons: First, people thirty-four and younger already occupy lower-, middle-, and even upper-management positions and will eventually be the top bosses, so their role in
change will prove crucial. Second, this age group usually is more
receptive to change than older categories. Third, there are so
many of them—2.7 million in their twenties in management jobs
now.

Many sympathetic but generally objective observers agree that
the junior managers are warmer and more open than their elders
but often extremely intense. They can be aggravating, even infu-
riating, to their supervisors because they tend to be sanctimonious. Their impatience makes some seem arrogant. They possess

competence and its corollary, self-confidence. They tend to over-state and overdo. With their lack of experience, they make mistakes in judgment. Little interested in the past, some of them have thought only superficially about business' potentials and limitations and expect more of it than it can deliver. Some of them are more concerned with how they're doing than with what they're doing.

They are generous and idealistic as a group, anxious to help others and willing to work hard for objectives they believe valid. They intend to shake the system until it changes and demand justifications for everything, including that most basic business principle, the profit motive.

Other experienced observers hold a somewhat different view of young people in business and industry. Peter Drucker has been watching (and influencing) management trends and practices for thirty years. He says this: "These kids go to college and then to business school. By the time they go to work after all that schooling, they are 25. In work experience they are the equivalent of the 15-year-old of a generation ago. But in theoretical knowledge they excel any one of their elders. So they go up fast—only to find themselves senior vice-presidents at the age of 29 but working for the same old bookkeeper I worked for years ago. . . .

"The young people today expect to see business run by theory, knowledge, concepts and planning. But then they find it is run like the rest of the world—by experience and expediency, by whom you know and by the hydrostatic pressure in your bladder. . . . We have an indiscriminate input of people who have been trained to use knowledge, but we haven't learned how to put them to work. . . ."

Drucker believes business really penalizes young managers with its present approach: "Nothing creates disaffection faster than a big title, a lot of money and only donkey work to do. It destroys your hope, because where else is there to go? The absence of demand, responsibility, and the chance to fail and achieve is very discouraging. Especially when you are surrounded by a sea of contemporaries in the same situation. They [young managers] are very vulnerable because so many of them have ridden too far, too fast. They haven't had a chance to learn enough about their jobs. Also a lot of them haven't enough compassion. They haven't learned that character is more important than abilities. A clash is definitely coming, but not between the old and the young—among the young people themselves."

Drucker and others worry about the age-distribution factor. Ten years or so from now, many young whiz kids of today will be about forty, all competing for the top job. Many won't make it. There will be a problem of finding second careers for people who have been successful very early but who by sheer arithmetic can go no further from where they are.

This matter of numbers already holds profound significance for the manager of change—an importance that will grow steadily for the next decade. Two important job requirements—steady work and important and significant work—will become more difficult to meet. Therefore, positive changes may grow more difficult to put into effect.

Another numbers factor that ultimately affects the management of change is the working life span. It's now forty to forty-five years vs. about thirty years in the teens of this century. This results from the longer life expectancy and improved health in later years. So more people in their late fifties and early sixties remain on the job today than fifty to fifty-five years ago. While many older people embrace change with as much or more enthusiasm than younger people, the majority probably do not. This poses a severe motivational problem to every manager of change.

What to do? Apply the principles and suggestions given here, with one additional proviso: Use compassion. To paraphrase the remark attributed to Mark Twain about his father: When you pay respectful attention to the veterans on the job, you may be surprised to discover how much they have learned since you talked to them a few years back.

THREE CASE STUDIES IN MOTIVATION

How does change usually get motivated in real life? Let's examine three case studies—in a profession, in a single company, and in one small component of a company.

Engineering, one of the glamour professions of the 1960s, came upon hard times in the 1970s. In April 1971 an estimated 65,000 engineers were unemployed out of about 1 million in the United States, largely because of deep cuts in defense, aerospace, and research and development. Grim as the employment story was, even deeper concerns existed; engineers felt they had been reduced to cogs in big organizational wheels. As many as 40 per cent of them would choose a different profession if they had a chance to start again.

But ambitious programs were underway to renovate the profession. Federal agencies, state governments, and engineering societies were retraining laid-off men for specialties in demand. At the engineering schools, new courses stressed the systems approach and the social impact of engineering projects. The schools were working closely with employers to combat the serious problems of early obsolescence. More engineers were waking up to the fact that it is not a virtue to remain aloof, that they must develop a greater sense of professionalism and take more responsibility for the changes they bring to the world.

It took a near-disaster to shake the engineering profession up. Unfortunately such drastic motivation sometimes proves necessary. But often techniques and programs are already in place to handle the change somewhat more neatly.

For instance, the same aerospace austerity led a defense-related company in California to a fairly radical reorganization in which it consolidated three divisions, added a new division, and made major managerial shifts.

At the time of the change in early 1971, the vice president of industrial relations predicted, "We think we will be better able to manage the change and get the company adjusted within months, instead of years."

His confidence was based on experience, not bravado. During the 1960s, the firm evolved a unique management style. It linked two intriguing and often controversial concepts: management by matrix where work is organized around temporary teams, and organization development which uses behavioral science techniques, such as sensitivity training and confrontation sessions, to make those teams operate more efficiently.

The vice president's confidence was not misplaced. The company weathered the storm well, its new organization contributing importantly to the success.

But most motivation-for-change experiences occur on a smaller scale. Typical is the case of twelve welders in General Electric's plant in Syracuse, New York.

The premise of an experiment was that if factory workers had a chance to make more personal contribution in their work, they would also give more personal commitment. Besides the welding work they normally performed, the group was also offered responsibility for the planning, scheduling, and control functions. They would receive the drawings and specifications, plan the job, sketch the tooling or fixturing, and communicate directly with managers and specialists in other areas when necessary. When they needed help, they could call on the foreman or any of the engineers and other experts who normally had performed the planning and other technical functions for welding operations. This help would be given, however, only at their request. Leadership would be provided from within the group.

The experiment worked out well.

"The men showed enthusiasm for their work," commented Dr. Herbert H. Meyer, GE's manager of personnel research. "Management showed trust in them and respect for them, and they reacted in a responsible and conscientious manner."

One direct result of the weld-team concept has been a substantial savings in overhead for the machine shop, plus overhead reductions in the planning and tooling areas.

Dr. Meyer adds: "The intensive guidance of a highly trained psychologist is not required to make substantial changes in the way the roles of hourly employees are defined in order to enhance their motivation. It does require considerable courage on the part of the managers involved."

The key to sound motivation is confidence. Confidence at all managerial levels is a must. If middle managers believe in their top managers, but in turn lack the confidence of their own people, the organization faces considerable trouble. But to go one step further, if middle management is disillusioned with top management, we're in even more trouble. Disillusionment with management in any institution breeds indifference. Then the mischief wrought by the half-done job from the halfhearted worker is incalculable.

Good motivation will go far to forestall such half-work, but it won't do everything. The multiplier manager must know the techniques of his job, too, to deal effectively with change. We'll turn next to the administrative aspects of managing innovation.

chapter nineteen

Administering Change

The dictionary defines futuriasis as "abnormal fixation or concern regarding that which is about to be, fear of the future."

If you read only Henry Kissinger, Charles Reich, Arthur Burns, Alvin Toffler, and Herman Kahn, for example, they might leave you with the impression that an epidemic of futuriasis was sweeping the country in the 1970s.

As the pace of change speeds up, many men respond by intensifying their forecasting and planning, by elaborating their alternatives—perhaps at the expense of the present. But managing change involves coping with the present so that the future may prove more profitable, both figuratively and literally. Much of that coping involves the mundane matter of administering change. We do not leave it until last because it holds the least importance. We bring it up now because it should be considered last chronologically.

CASE STUDY: ABC CORPORATION

Consider the administrative phases involved in that typical business change, the introduction of a new product. ABC Corporation's experiences illustrate the problems. In the early years of this century, the company made fare boxes for street cars and buses. When this faltered, it entered the timer business for appliances in the 1930s. After World War II, it found that its customers, the manufacturers of appliances, turned to making their own timers. So ABC went into its own line of home and industrial timers in the late 1940s.

The retelling sounds simple, but just the administration of such changes, omitting all other considerations, entailed formidable complexity. For instance, before each major product shift ABC had to:

■ Establish a good sales organization and establish a sales-promotion program.

■ Rewrite product literature and issue new catalogs.

■ Determine product costs and improve efficiency to compete in a market where it was a comparative latecomer.

■ Arrange to reengineer some aspects of the products.

■ Effect basic personnel changes, including some shifts among executive ranks, to deal effectively with a new business.

■ Reduce the overhead.

■ Set new product standards.

■ Establish employee training programs to help production-line and other people learn to make the new products.

■ Determine what equipment was necessary to produce the new products and acquire that which it did not already possess.

■ Arrange, if necessary, for the financing to acquire such equipment.

We need not carry this listing further to see that the successful manager of change must be a good administrator. The dictionary defines an administrator as "one who manages affairs." Here we use the term in the sense of one who can get the activities moving that make change take place. So when it comes to innovation, the manager of change must have creative abilities in two areas—doing and thinking. There's the rub, because the two activities don't always go together.

Although change-minded people generally tend more to thinking than doing (or vice versa), the qualities don't necessarily have to be mutually antagonistic. An example to illustrate how the twin activities of change can be combined in one person lies in the careers of two highly innovative men who both contributed greatly to change in all our lives—Einstein and Edison.

Because of an indifferent academic record, Albert Eistein failed to find a teaching job and had to settle for a minor position as a junior patent examiner in Berne, Switzerland. Yet the job left him time to contemplate fundamental problems in physics. His contemplations led to applications, including nuclear power, of monumental impact. The applications, however, came largely from others. While Einstein was primarily a thinker, Thomas Edison was largely an inspired doer or applier of others' basic ideas. One of his justly memorable phrases in reply to the query as to whether he was a genius: "Genius is ninety-nine per cent perspiration and one per cent inspiration."

He always had reserve ideas. "If that doesn't work," he would say, "we'll try this."

Yet the ideal manager of change somehow combines the roles of thinker and doer. On occasion, Edison could do this. He had the habit of taking catnaps and frequently emerged from sleep with new ideas. He grew so preoccupied with his interior thoughts at times that once when he was standing in line to pay taxes at New York City Hall, he forgot his own name as the clerk called it and lost his place in the queue. He probably exaggerated his deafness to avoid distractions.

And Einstein could combine his otherworldliness at times with a surprising practicality. When he lived in Princeton, New Jersey, many refugees from Hitler's Germany grew grateful for his realistic aid. He helped neighbors' children with their arithmetic homework and played the violin with professional skill.

All managers of change must learn some of the skills of doing to become successful in implementing ideas. When the researcher Charles F. Kettering had ready a quick-drying enamel lacquer for automobiles, he encountered opposition to it from some of his associates at General Motors. One day, he invited his principal opponent to lunch and arranged for a long meal. When the two finally emerged, Kettering's opponent found his car parked at the curb glistening in a fresh—and dry—coat of paint. Then and there, the head of GM's research had accomplished the task of winning his battle for the quick-drying finish.

THE JOB BEFORE YOU

But most cases of administration of change prove more mundane. The function of your work lies mainly in one or more of five areas—manufacturing, engineering, finance, marketing, or personnel. Let's consider the task of "doing" in each.

Manufacturing. Figures taken from an in-depth study of five manufacturing plants made by the Connecticut management consulting firm Gemar Associates, Inc., revealed that they were chugging along at about 50 per cent of maximum labor productivity. "The inefficiency," says Gemar president Robert J. Andersen, Jr., "is due primarily to companies not keeping pace with changing production conditions, like product mix, volume, manufacturing methods, and quality standards. Simply, companies usually don't do enough periodic reviewing of their facilities and staffing to insure maximum efficiency."

He noted one of the best ways to "do something" about productivity is to audit plant operations—an administrative action. This can be anything from spot-checking work at various places in a plant to a large-scale analysis of all plant operations. Much about plant efficiency—or inefficiency—can usually be learned by an informal audit plus work sampling.

The informal audit involves nothing more than a walk through the plant with stops and critical looks at points where problems are apparent. For instance, a machine where an unusual back-up of orders exists calls for a stop and a look. Or a work area passed by several times without any apparent activity going on. Why not?

Any audit, regardless of scale, should include a hard look at indirect labor as well as at direct labor—another administrative step.

Time your audit after major changes in product mix take place and audit prior to making major capital commitments.

And intensive work sampling—still another administrative move—made before money is put on the line for new equipment can often be a management eye opener.

"In our work," says Andersen, "we sometimes find claimed needs for new equipment are due to poor management and planning rather than to an actual shortage of proper equipment."

Engineering. A plant manager wished to reduce the downtime of his expensive equipment. He achieved his aim as the result of a creative bit of administration. Because of the complexity of the machines, he had assigned maintenance responsibilities to the engineering department. But the engineers had many other things to do, so the preventive maintenance sometimes didn't get accomplished as planned, eventually resulting in more emergency maintenance situations.

His solution: Train a group of intelligent hourly employees to do maintenance work full time on the automated equipment. In his employee newspaper, he advertised for people interested in joining a training program. Forty-eight applied. Eleven passed qualifying aptitude and achievement tests. He chose seven for a one-year course that cost his company $75,000 to conduct. The gamble paid off handsomely. The company now has seven capable maintenance men for automation equipment. The program improved the morale of hourly employees and saved the engineers for other valuable work.

Finance. An accountant with a degree fresh from a California university began working for a steel-warehousing firm with distribution centers in three cities. All accounting was done centrally —"for reasons of centralized efficiency," growled the manager when the accountant asked.

Yet the new man noted that one warehouse dealt only with stainless-steel products; another handled just tubing; a third specialized in steel building-trades products. Customers differed at each location; each unit's billing practices varied; each experienced individual finance problems. Although the top management prided itself on its centralized system, it actually had to deal with each unit separately.

The new accountant persisted in proposing an administrative change: A separate finance operation at each location, with an accountant in charge on the spot, but responsible to the chief finance man at the home office. Finally management agreed to try the idea—and saved $30,000 in the first full year of decentralization because of faster billing and reduced paperwork.

Marketing. Remember Pareto's law? A market researcher did in making a change for an industrial supplier. He found that 80 per cent of the sales went to 20 per cent of the customers. What's more, he learned that 5 per cent of the sales generated losses, not profits, because the low volume didn't justify the expense of selling. His administrative suggestion: Eliminate the 5 per cent of loss sales. Use the salesman's time usually devoted to them in missionary work to boost the volume from the customers who bought in profitable, but only moderate, volume. Within a year, the company's total sales had increased by one-third even though it had dropped the 5 per cent portion of its sales that had proved unprofitable.

Personnel. A midwestern company became concerned about rising absenteeism among its employees. It decided to shift from the conventional five-day, forty-hour week to a four-day, forty-hour week, with three days off per week. The innovation worked; its absenteeism declined by nearly 75 per cent; its turnover dropped (an unlooked for benefit), and its productivity climbed by 20 per cent.

But this shift involved many administrative considerations. For example:

■ During its feasibility study, it decided to involve only the top managers to minimize the possibility of leakage. But when it decided to go ahead with the shift, it involved middle managers and supervisors—a group at a time, evaluating the reaction of each.

■ It announced the decision to employees in small groups, provided a document spelling out the schedule and how it would affect them, and asked for questions pertaining to the document.

■ It allowed three weeks to study the move, a week to discuss and communicate it, and a week to monitor the plan after implementation.

■ Although it had no union, it weighed the possibilities of unionization if the plan failed. It decided to take the risk.

■ The midwestern company management examined the payroll in detail in terms of unit costs, overtime, and benefits.

■ It looked at absenteeism and turnover on a month-to-month basis by departments to see if something else—working conditions, for example—spurred the absenteeism. It couldn't pinpoint anything definite, which confirmed it in its decision to try the four-day week.

■ It canvassed employee opinion, because if the workers did not want it there was no use trying it.

■ It looked at its policies on rest periods and lunch hour and decided to keep the rest breaks but reduce the lunch hour to thirty minutes. It turned up the obvious, but often overlooked, fact that you eliminate 20 per cent of break time on a four-day schedule.

■ It examined production bottlenecks and machine downtime schedules because scheduling is more critical in a four-day than in a five-day cycle.

■ It decided that public-dealing units of the business—primarily sales, shipping, and receiving components—should stay on five days, the standard schedule for most of the working world.

■ It considered employees' commuting distances, car-pool arrangements and traffic situations at the starting and closing times.

■ It considered—but rejected—the possibility of giving an attendance bonus, believing that the three days off per week constituted sufficient incentive.

■ It established a holiday policy based on the ten-hour rather than the eight-hour day.

In all these examples, the managers of change took the following five basic steps in their administration of the changes:

1. They adjusted to the problem.
2. They got the facts.
3. They hunted for ideas that oriented with both the facts and the problems.
4. They let the change idea simmer.
5. They appraised the ideas.

We'll look at each step in administration in detail.

ADJUSTING TO THE PROBLEM

Becoming familiar with the difficulty often proves the greatest challenge in administering change. For instance, the marketing researcher made false starts because he initially considered his problem a low profit ratio. Although that was troublesome, the correct orientation turned out to be too many unprofitable sales. When he saw this, he quickly came up with the correct administrative innovation.

Sometimes the problem appears so obvious that you attempt too obvious—and uncreative—solutions. A common approach to absenteeism is exhortation. The midwestern firm took a less obvious solution, the four-day week, and found it brilliantly successful.

Occasionally, you may not realize that a problem exists. Questions of productivity sometimes fall into this area. You slip unknowingly into sloppy habits, as Gemar's Andersen points out.

At other times, the true problem remains disoriented because too many people accept current dogma. The manager for the warehousing firm had that trouble. It delayed him in accepting the recent graduate's suggestion for decentralizing accounting because he had unquestioningly accepted the premise that all centralization leads to greater efficiency.

Accepted solutions lie in this category, too. Nobody questioned the plant manager's decision to have his engineers maintain complex automated equipment because other factory managers took the same administrative approach. Because this manager looked deeper and broader than usual, he developed a more perceptive solution.

To orient your problem:

■ List every factor you can think of that could be part of the problem.

■ Put in writing what you think the problem is. Express it in as many ways as come to mind. Select the best expression or combination of expressions.

■ Rearrange the factors into a logical relationship to what the problem is. Set the sequences, and look for the key factor.

■ Try to explain it orally to someone unfamiliar with the problem.

■ Ask questions of anyone involved with the problem and those perceptive people unfamiliar with it.

■ Divide the problem into as small parts as possible.

■ Concentrate your administrative activities on those parts that you can control.

OBTAINING THE FACTS

No matter how complex, all human thought processes rely on facts. The in-depth study of productivity in five manufacturing plants aimed at finding facts on the subject. The plant manager with automated equipment needed facts on maintenance before he could make administrative changes in his maintenance program. The young graduate looked at readily available facts with a fresh eye. The market researcher had to find the facts about sales costs. The midwestern company's personnel manager unearthed facts about why employees were absent.

Once armed with the facts, you must use them imaginatively, as the managers of change did in the cases cited. And you must get as many of the facts as practicable. The market researcher could have stopped with the fact that 20 per cent of his company's sales generated 80 per cent of the volume. If he had, he would have missed the key fact—that 5 per cent of the sales were at a loss.

Another challenge lies in the facts' validity. Imagine the repercussions if, for example, the midwestern company had shifted to a four-day week, only to discover that a majority of the employees didn't want it.

HUNTING FOR IDEAS

Two fundamental routes lie before you as you search for administrative ideas to implement change. First, you can start with the known, existing idea, select one of its characteristics, and change it to make it into something new. The work week once was six days, then five and a half days, and now commonly five. The common characteristic is days of work. Why not change the five-day week to a four-day week? The midwestern company did and administered a dramatic change.

The other normal way to get ideas is the opposite of the first.

Start with the unknown and work backwards. The manager with maintenance problems knew he had excessive downtime. Why? He worked backwards, to discover that his engineers didn't have the time to perform enough preventive maintenance. That led to his successful plan to train hourly people as maintenance men.

If you go this second road, problem orientation will be vital. This leads to three steps in following this path to new ideas. First, know what you seek. You cannot go far with general objectives, such as "I want to reduce downtime." You will do better to say, "I want to find out why I have so much downtime and solve that problem in such a way that I can better utilize all my people."

Second, analyze your contemplated administrative change's dominant quality. For example, the dominant aspect of the maintenance problem is really not downtime as such. It is better utilization of people. You start from there.

Third, analyze the attributes of your planned change. With utilization of people as the prime quality in the maintenance problem, you go to characteristics of people utilization. Does it make sense to use expensive engineers for maintenance, especially when they are so busy with other matters that interest them more? Does it make sense not to use intelligent hourly people who would jump at the higher pay and prestige of maintenance work? The answer to both questions was an unqualified no, and the administrative change developed logically.

A series of self-questions such as the following may help you make more and better administrative changes:

Can an idea be put to another use? The audit is a common financial tool. Why not try it in manufacturing situations to check on productivity?

Can you adapt an idea? Does the past offer parallels? What or whom can you copy or emulate? The same arguments advanced for the five-day week in the 1930s are being offered for the four-day week now.

Can you modify the idea? Give it a new twist or change its

meaning? The accountant applied Pareto's law and discovered even more than the 80:20 ratio. He added another number, 5, the percentage of unprofitable sales.

Can you magnify the idea? The conventional financial audit gets greatly expanded in determining productivity ratios in a manufacturing environment.

Can you subtract from the idea? Omit something from it? Decentralization in accounting implies complete home rule, but the accountant in the warehousing firm recommended keeping a centralized financial chief supervising the individuals responsible at local plants.

Can you substitute one thing for another in the idea? The manufacturing manager substituted hourly people for engineers as his maintenance men.

Can you rearrange the idea? When the steel-warehousing firm changed from centralized to decentralized accounting, it rearranged the idea to come up with a new creation.

Can you combine ideas? The market researcher combined the Pareto idea with the notion that some sales brought losses, not profits.

LETTING IDEAS SIMMER

You need to mature and to fill out your ideas. Complex ideas, particularly, deserve such treatment. Matthew Arnold, the nineteenth-century English writer and critic, said, "Our ideas will, in the end, shape the world better for maturing a little."

To decentralize its financial operation, the steel distributor experienced "debugging" problems, particularly in the selection of the right accountant for each location. The marketing researcher met strong resistance at first to his idea about abandoning the unprofitable 5 per cent of sales. Only when he considered what could be done to make up for the loss did he refine his idea sufficiently to sell it.

To let your ideas simmer:

- Let them sit in your notebook or on your tape for a least a few days. Then return to them to see if they still look as good.
- Apply some of the questions suggested in the section on searching for ideas, to learn if you can improve your approach to administrative change.
- Distinguish between fussing with and improving an idea. Endless tinkering may lead to senility, not maturity, in your creation.
- Accept constructive suggestion. Some managers of change suffer from the NIH (not invented here) disease and refuse contributions from anyone else.

APPRAISING THE IDEAS

You take three basic steps in evaluating ideas—generally ranking them, tightly ranking them according to general criteria, and consideration of possible improvements in each.

When you have done this, you need to turn to analysis on another level. How much trouble will the idea cause to put into effect? The case-study ideas considered here all proved worth the trouble. Yet others may not. Management of a Los Angeles–based company rejected in April the proposal to change the vacation shutdown from the first two weeks in August to the last two weeks in June because the shift would have caused too much trouble over employees' previously made plans. Finance personnel had made the suggestion to facilitate a special mid-year inventory.

How fast can you make the change effective? Occasionally the idea loses value because of timing, as in the case of the vacation rescheduling. Yet, you may enhance the value of a change by shifting its timing. The steel distributor believed it needed about six months to plan for the decentralization, but it had two other reorganizations to go into effect almost immediately. It decided that all should take place at once, so it delayed the other two and speeded up its decentralization so that everything meshed.

How costly is the change to implement? The $75,000 expense of the maintenance training program almost undid it, but the manufacturing manager developed figures to show that the conventional methods of maintenance would cost even more.

You cope with the present to deal effectively with the future. Administering change often boils down to common-sense basics applied now. For example, consider an analogy. Forest Rangers, Boy Scouts, and other outdoor people give these four rules for survival if you get lost in the wilderness:

1. Stay calm. Panic accounts for 90 per cent of the problem.
2. Stay in one place. Don't go off in all directions. You will get nowhere.
3. Keep dry and warm.
4. Have the will to live.

These four rules can also be applied to survival in the face of change:

1. Stay calm. Panic will avail you nothing. The change may benefit you.
2. Appraise the situation with hard thought. Where do you want the change to take you?
3. Some principles and convictions—honesty, compassion, etc. —never change. Hang on to them no matter what else is changing.
4. Have the will to survive. Listless resignation to change will not help you prosper with the change. Seek to control it, not to let it control you.

Index

Index